Merry!
Christmas 1997
To: Bruce
From Lane & Walter

# WILD GAME COOKING

# WILD GAME COOKING

## Jonquil & Edward Barr

### Illustrations by Sarah Hocombe

ROSENDALE PRESS

**For the friends who helped**

First published in Great Britain in 1988 by:
Rosendale Press Ltd, 140 Rosendale Road
London SE21 8LG

Cover design by Robert Budwig
Artwork & Production, Pep Reiff
Printed in England by Billing & Sons Ltd., Worcester

ISBN 0 9509182 5 3

# Acknowledgements

To have a dinner party with partridge or pigeon cooked in three different ways and to enjoy, or otherwise, tasting from each other's plates, assessing and commenting was great fun but it does need patience and forebearance on the part of one's guests. This is why we can say, with feeling, that without the help of family and friends this book would never have been completed. There are many others whose help we are glad to acknowledge.

First among these is Maureen Green, whose idea this book was, who has thoughtfully edited what we have written and kept us strictly to a schedule. We must also thank Ulf and Nadine Stelzenmüller, who have kindly supplied recipes from Germany, Claudine Siegenthaler, a Swiss entomologist who loves food almost as much as insects, Marie-Madeleine Jacquemier at whose home in the Jura we have eaten as well as we have anywhere. Piers and Judith Bastard gave us an idea for guinea fowl, Sally Harrison inspired venison recipes and Elke Vollstedt of Frankfurt kindly allowed us to use her wild boar speciality. Our thanks also to Diane Seed for the hare recipe from, 'The Top 100 Pasta Sauces'.

Peter Gray, chairman of the British Deer Farmers Association, answered our many questions on venison. Among suppliers we would like to thank Sam Weller of 'The Wild Boar Company', 8 Owen Mansions, Queens Club Gardens, London W.14 and Stephen Andrade of David Andrade and Sons Ltd. of Smithfield Market, who supplied us with kid meat. Tony and Maggie Laing of 'Maggie's Game Shop' near Battle have not only generously advised us on many technical issues but have supplied the greater part of the game we have cooked.

Among restauranteurs who have kindly parted with some of their special recipes, we would like to thank Graham Beauchamp of 'Rules', London, Alasdair Robertson of The Holly Tree Hotel, Argyll, Scotland; Sauro Brunicardi of 'La Mora' in Ponte a Moriano in Tuscany; and Julien of 'La Chaumière' in Lauris-sur-Durance in Provence.

# CONTENTS

# INTRODUCTION

Game is still something of a rare experience for many food enthusiasts, but today there is every reason why it should make more frequent appearances on the table. Not only is it good for those in search of a healthy, low-fat diet, but it is more widely available in supermarkets.

As meat, game is full of flavour but mercifully free from the growth hormones and other additives that now arouse such anxiety about factory-farmed animals. Because birds and animals such as pigeon, pheasant, rabbit and venison lead healthy lives with natural exercise, their flesh is lean and appealing to those who want to avoid excessive animals fats.

And, as an ingredient, game meat is now much more readily to hand. Supermarkets stock fresh venison, pheasant and partridge through the winter months, while pigeon, mallard duck, rabbit, quail and guinea fowl are available all the year round. Venison, once only available from hunted animals of indeterminate age, is now on the market chiefly as farm-bred meat, produced with careful farming methods, and the flesh itself is more consistent in quality and age. New choices, such as kid and wild boar, are coming on to the market, although they still need seeking out.

Speciality game shops not only stock many game birds and animals in their season, but now often run an extensive deep-freeze. And, as Elizabeth David remarked many years ago, in *French Provincial Cooking*, the 'deep freeze is kinder to game than to vegetables, meat or fish.'

The only disadvantage is, perhaps, that many game meats, apart from rabbit and pigeon, are marginally more expensive than more conventional protein from the average butcher or supermarket. This is bound to be so for any meat that is not produced by mass market methods. But, for those who are cutting down on the amount of meat that they eat, to pay a little more for high-protein, low-fat varieties can still seem like good value.

Unfamiliarity alone may be a deterrent. Venison, in many minds, is associated with Robin Hood or the royal table. Yet in Germany it is a staple luxury, no more exotic than chocolate cake. Both pheasant and rabbit are sometimes victims of snobbery, one considered too grand, the other too humble for the average table. But pheasant, a Middle Eastern bird introduced into western Europe by the Romans, can be cooked as simply or as elaborately as chicken. And rabbit has never been despised either by French or Italian cooks, who have invented roasts and casseroles, pâtés and terrines to use its low-fat meat.

The only problem in reality is that all meat that is so very lean needs to be cooked with care. Hanging game until the rot sets in, in other words until it is tenderized by bacteria, no longer finds favour from the health or practical point of view, since comparatively few of us now shoot our own game. Brutal over-cooking can be a disaster; under-cooking and then 'resting' the meat in a warm oven is always to be preferred. For all dry meat, either fats or liquids are essential to make them succulent. Hence the importance of marinating game meat, and per-meating the flesh with acid liquids such as wine, vinegar and lemon juice. Some herbs, such as garlic, and fruits such as kiwi fruit, papaya or mango contain enzymes which tenderize meat fibres. Oil is a benefit on grilled (broiled meats) and other small joints. And larding (or making small inserts, called barding) with pork fat is a traditional method of adding some tenderizing fat. Basting with oil and wine is recommended in many recipes.

Marinades have other purposes, too. Steeping meat in a mixture of wine, oil and herbs helps to offset strong flavours and distribute them. Most marinades can then be used in the cooking, although the German wild boar recipe on page 92 specifically states that it must be discarded since the flavour extracted from the boar meat will be too powerful.

From a nutritionist's point of view, the dense, high-protein meat of game birds and animals is ideal food, provided that some allowance is made for the lack of fibre that all meats suffer from. For this reason among others, some of the accompaniments recommended with the game recipes in this book are rice, Rösti, and pasta, not the traditional garnishes of tiny potato 'shoe strings'. A good range of vegetables is, in fact, a highly recommended accompaniment to all game dishes, as well as the sharp fruit and jelly flavourings that are so delicious a complement.

Although many of those who have turned to vegetarianism over the last few years, whether for reasons of health to avoid animal fats, or to avoid the meat additives and brutality of factory farming methods, may not easily be won back, nutritionist and metabolic counsellor, Robert Erdmann, tells his patients, 'if you must eat meat, game is much to be preferred'.

Many others, good cooks and enthusiastic eaters, will concur. If you want to eat meat, eat meat that tastes like meat. Go for game.

## NOTE

**Although there is no substitute for the flavour of butter in cooking, many who are interested in the low fat properties of game may prefer to substitute a vegetable margarine, high in poly-unsaturates and low in cholesterol for butter, to reduce the animal fat content of the recipes even further.**

# RABBIT

Rabbit is one meat freely available throughout the year, fresh as well as frozen.

Wild rabbits are shot or they can be ferreted, to avoid shot in the meat. Wild rabbits have a stronger flavour than hutch or domesticated rabbit specially bred for the table and unless they are young, preferably three to four months, are noticeably tougher.

Frozen rabbit, commonly farmed in China, is what is most frequently available in supermarkets and butchers. Don't underrate it, it can be delicious. Indeed wild rabbit, we think, can often have too strong a taste and for some dishes such as those with a cream based sauce we prefer hutch rabbit — the flavour is more delicate and the flesh paler. We usually soak all rabbit, tame or wild, for 12 hours or overnight in a mixture of either vinegar or lemon or salt and water.

Rabbit is an economical meat to buy, partly because in Britain and the United States, there has long been a prejudice against it. In our opinion, this is well worth overcoming to enjoy some of the many and varied rabbit recipes found in all culinary traditions.

Wild rabbit always takes longer to cook than hutch rabbit, as we have indicated in the recipes.

# Rabbit stir-fry with sweetcorn and water chestnuts
### Serves 4

| METRIC/IMPERIAL | U.S. |
|---|---|
| 450 g/1 lb boneless rabbit | 1 lb |
| 3 cloves of garlic | 3 |
| 35 g/1¼ oz peeled fresh root ginger | 1¼ oz |
| 2 medium carrots | 2 |
| 150 g/5 oz baby sweetcorn | 5 oz |
| 1 sweet red pepper | 1 |
| 225 g/8 oz canned water chestnuts, drained | 8 oz (⅔ cup) |
| 75-90 ml/5-6 tbsp sunflower oil | 5-6 tbsp |
| 100 g/4 oz peas, fresh | ¾ cup |
| 75 g/3 oz bean sprouts | 3 oz (¾ cup) |
| 50 g/2 oz shelled cashew nuts | ⅓ cup |
| fine sea salt and freshly ground black pepper | |
| SAUCE | |
| 60 ml/4 tbsp soy sauce | ¼ cup |
| 30 ml/2 tbsp dry sherry | 2 tbsp |
| 10 ml/2 tsp brown sugar | 2 tsp |
| 10 ml/2 tsp white wine vinegar | 2 tsp |
| 7.5 ml/1½ tsp cornflour (cornstarch) | 1½ tsp |

Mix together the sauce ingredients. Before beginning to cook prepare all the ingredients: cut the rabbit into 2.5 cm/1 inch cubes. Finely chop the garlic and ginger; cut the carrots and sweet corn into 5 mm/¼ inch slanting slices; remove the seeds and pith from the red pepper and cut it into matchsticks; slice the water chestnuts. Each ingredient should be kept separate. Assemble everything in an orderly fashion nearby.
A wok is the best utensil for stir-frying as the contents tumble together in the hottest part, but a good-sized heavy-bottomed frying pan will do almost as well.
Place the pan over the highest heat possible. When it is hot, add 30 ml/2 tbsp of the oil and heat until it ripples when the pan is tipped. As soon as the oil is ready, add the ginger and garlic. Stir and toss until lightly browned. Add the rabbit cubes in two batches, stirring and tossing until lightly browned (2−3 minutes). As the cubes are browned, remove and keep warm.

Put in the rest of the oil, heat and add the vegetables, one variety at a time, and cashew nuts in the order listed above. Continue to stir and fry the vegetables and nuts until they are coated with oil and thoroughly mixed together (2–3 minutes). Season to taste with salt and pepper. Return the rabbit to the pan. Mix well with the vegetables and add the sauce. Stir-fry until the sauce thickens and flavours the dish. Serve immediately on hot plates.

# Rabbit in mustard sauce
(Lapin aux deux moutardes)
Serves 4

| METRIC/IMPERIAL | U.S. |
|---|---|
| 1 rabbit | 1 |
| vinegar | |
| flour | |
| fine sea salt and freshly ground black pepper | |
| 45 ml/3 tbsp olive oil | 3 tbsp |
| 175 g/6 oz smoked bacon | 6oz |
| 6 shallots | 6 |
| 300 ml/½ pint white or rosé wine | 1¼ cups |
| 150 ml/¼ pint chicken stock | ⅔ cup |
| 1 bouquet garni | 1 |
| 5 ml/1 tsp prepared English mustard | 1 tsp |
| 10 ml/ 2 tsp whole grain Moutarde de Meaux | 2 tsp |
| 300 ml/½ pint single (light) cream or | |
| plain yoghurt | 1¼ cups |

Cut the rabbit into joints and soak overnight in vinegar water. Drain, rinse in fresh water and pat dry. Roll in flour seasoned with salt and pepper. Heat the oil in a saucepan or flameproof casserole, add the rabbit and the diced bacon and brown well. Slice the shallots and add them together with the white wine, stock and bouquet garni. Cover with a double layer of foil and put the lid on tightly. Leave to simmer gently for about 1½-2 hours, even longer for wild rabbit. Remove the rabbit and keep it warm. Skim the cooking liquid if you feel there is excess fat, add the two mustards with the cream or yoghurt and stir in very gently. Taste for seasoning. The sauce should be fairly sharp. Put the rabbit on a serving dish and pour the sauce over.

15

# Young roast rabbit on a bed of onions
### Serves 4

| METRIC/IMPERIAL | U.S. |
|---|---|
| 1 rabbit | 1 |
| 22 ml/1½ tbsp mild olive oil | 1½ tbsp |
| 450 g/1 lb onions | 1 lb |
| 300 ml/½ pint cider (hard apple cider) | 1¼ cups |
| fine sea salt and freshly ground black pepper | |
| 8 small sausages | 8 |
| STUFFING | |
| 1 medium onion | 1 |
| 50-75 g/2-3 oz streaky (fatty)bacon | 2-3 oz |
| 22 ml/1½ tbsp mild olive oil | 1½ tbsp |
| 75 g/3 oz fresh wholemeal breadcrumbs | 1½ cups |
| 10 ml/2 tsp dried thyme | 2 tsp |
| 60 ml/4 tbsp freshly chopped parsley | ¼ cup |
| 50 g/2 oz shredded beef or vegetable suet | 2 oz (¼ cup) |
| grated rind of ½ lemon | |
| fine sea salt and freshly ground black pepper | |
| 1 egg | 1 |

Prepare the stuffing first. Finely chop the onion, and cut the bacon into small dice. Fry in the oil until the onion is soft and the bacon fat runs a little. Remove from the heat and add the breadcrumbs, thyme and parsley. Gently stir together. Put the onion and bacon mixture into a small bowl and add the suet, grated lemon rind, and salt and pepper to taste. Bind together with the beaten egg. Mix well.

Preheat the oven to 200°C/400°F/Mark 6. Rinse the rabbit and pat dry. Fill the rabbit cavity with the stuffing and either sew together or close with skewers. Pour the oil into a small roasting pan and add the onions which you have sliced. Add the rabbit, cider, and salt and pepper to taste. Cover with foil and roast in the oven for about 1¼-2 hours. Baste the rabbit frequently with the liquid in the bottom of the pan, and if it looks as if it is drying out, add more oil. Remove the foil for the last 15 minutes so as to brown the rabbit well. Grill (broil) the sausages, and serve with the rabbit.

# Rabbit stuffed with herbs
(Coniglio farcito agli aromi)
Serves 4-6

| METRIC/IMPERIAL | U.S. |
|---|---|
| 200 g/7 oz lean boneless veal | 7 oz |
| 100 g/3½ oz soft white bread | 3 large slices |
| warm milk | |
| good bunch of parsley and chervil | |
| freshly grated nutmeg | |
| fine sea salt and freshly ground black pepper | |
| 20 g/¾ oz freshly grated Parmesan cheese | ¼ cup |
| 2 eggs | 2 |
| 1 rabbit | 1 |

This recipe is a speciality of La Mora restaurant, a superb, small restaurant north of Lucca in Tuscany, and the chef had kindly allowed us to reproduce it.

Preheat the oven to 150°C/300°F/Mark 2.
Finely chop or process the veal. Soak the bread in warm milk to soften it, then squeeze out excess milk and add the bread to the veal with the chopped herbs. The mixture should be a good green colour. Season well with nutmeg, salt and pepper to taste and then add the Parmesan cheese. Bind with the beaten eggs.
Split the rabbit open down the back and remove the bones.
Spread out the rabbit flesh and flatten it, then spread the veal stuffing over the whole. Roll up the rabbit into as neat a roll as possible and tie with soft string.
Wrap in greased foil and place in a roasting tin.
Cook in the oven for about 30-45 minutes, not much more.
When the rabbit is done (test with a skewer for clear juices), slice it into neat rounds and lay these on a hot serving dish.
This is delicious hot or cold.

# Provencal-style rabbit

(Lapin provencal)

Serves 4

| METRIC/IMPERIAL | U.S. |
|---|---|
| 1 rabbit | 1 |
| vinegar or lemon juice | |
| fine sea salt and freshly ground black pepper | |
| olive oil for frying | |
| 1 sweet red pepper | 1 |
| 1 sweet green pepper | 1 |
| 1-2 courgettes (zucchini) | 1-2 |
| 2 medium onions | 2 |
| 2 cloves of garlic | 2 |
| 4 large ripe tomatoes | 4 |
| or | |
| 400 g/14 oz canned tomatoes | 14 oz |
| 4 sprigs of fresh thyme or lemon thyme | 4 |
| or | |
| 5 ml/1 tsp dried thyme | 1 tsp |
| handful of stoned black olives. | |

We doubt if this economical dish is strictly from Provence, but we enjoyed it there frequently in both winter and summer.

Cut the rabbit into joints and soak overnight in salted , vinegar or lemon water. Drain, rinse in fresh water and pat dry.
Preheat the oven to 20°C/250°F/Mark 1-2.
Pour a small amount of olive oil into a small, flameproof casserole, just enough to coat the bottom of the dish, and heat it. Roll the pieces of rabbit in the oil and brown them on all sides. Cut the peppers in half and remove the pith and seeds. Cut the peppers into long thin strips, and the courgette (zucchini) into chunky rounds. Chop the onions and garlic into chunks. Add all the prepared vegetables to the casserole. Mix in the tomatoes (if using fresh tomatoes, add a little water and chop the tomatoes into thick slices). Add the thyme, and salt and pepper to taste. Bring to the boiling point on top of the stove, then cover the casserole with a double layer of foil, press the lid on firmly and transfer to the oven. Cook for about 1½ hours for hutch rabbit, 2½ hours for wild rabbit. If the stew starts to look as if it is drying out, add more water. Remove the foil and the lid for the last 20

minutes of cooking and stir in 30 ml/2 tbsp of good olive oil and the olives. Adjust the seasoning before serving.

A fairly thick mush of delicious Provencal vegetables will surround the rabbit. You can, of course, add extra olive oil; as we have a passion for olives, a handful often stretches to two.

# Rabbit pie Maximoise
### Serves 4

| METRIC/IMPERIAL | U.S. |
|---|---|
| 1 rabbit | 1 |
| 1 stalk of young celery | 1 |
| 2 medium onions | 2 |
| 175 g/6 oz smoked bacon | 6 oz |
| 10 ml/2 tsp dried mixed herbs, such as sage, | |
| thyme, majoram, oregano, | 2 tsp |
| 1 bay leaf | 1 |
| fine sea salt and freshly ground black pepper | |
| 1½ wine glasses of Noilly Prat | |
| or other dry vermouth | 1½ wine glasses |
| good strong chicken stock | |
| short pastry, made with 225 g/8 oz (1⅔ cups)flour | |
| see page 117 | |
| 1 egg | 1 |

Preheat the oven to 220°C/425°F/Mark 7.

Cut the rabbit into joints and put into a pie dish together with the celery cut into small pieces, the onions roughly chopped and the bacon diced. Sprinkle with the mixed herbs and roll the rabbit pieces in this mixture. Add the bay leaf, salt and pepper to taste and vermouth. Add 2 tablespoons concentrated chicken stock. Cover with the pastry and decorate to your own design. Brush the top with beaten egg and make several small incisions in the pastry to let out the steam.

Bake for 20-25 minutes or until the pastry begins to brown, then turn the oven down to 170-180°C/325-350°F/Mark 3-4. Cover the pie with wet greaseproof (parchment) paper to stop the pastry from burning and bake for a further 1¼-1½ hours or until done. We usually heat a little extra chicken stock, laced with Noilly Prat, to add as extra gravy when serving the pie.

# Rabbit stew with parsley dumplings
### Serves 4

| METRIC/IMPERIAL | U.S. |
|---|---|
| 1 rabbit | 1 |
| fine sea salt and freshly ground black pepper | |
| flour | |
| 175 g/6 oz smoked bacon | 6 oz |
| 3 small carrots | 3 |
| 2 small turnips | 2 |
| 2 small onions | 2 |
| 22 ml/1½ tbsp sunflower oil for frying | 1½ tbsp |
| 2 cloves | 2 |
| 6 black peppercorns | 6 |
| 300 ml/½ pint cider (hard apple cider) | 1¼ cups |
| 300 ml/½ pint good stock | 1¼ cups |
| 1 bouquet garni | 1 |
| 50-100 g/2-4 oz green peas, fresh or frozen | ⅓-⅔ cup |
| 50-100 g/2-4 oz mushrooms | 2-4 oz |
| SUET DUMPLINGS | |
| 250 g/8 oz self-raising flour | 1 ⅔ cups |
| 5 ml/1 tsp fine sea salt | 1 tsp |
| 125 g/4 oz shredded beef or vegetable suet | 4 oz (½ cup) |
| freshly chopped parsley | |
| 120 ml/4 fl oz cold water | ½ cup |

Cut the rabbit into joints and soak overnight in salted water. Rinse well in clean water and pat dry. Roll in flour seasoned with salt and pepper.

Dice the bacon. Cut the carrots and turnips into small pieces. Slice the onions. Fry the onions gently in a little oil in a frying pan until soft but not brown, then remove and reserve. Add the bacon to the pan, fry until the fat runs; remove and reserve. Fry the rabbit pieces in the same fat until brown on all sides, transfer them to a saucepan. Add the onions, bacon, carrots, turnips, cloves, peppercorns, cider and stock, bouquet garni, and salt and pepper to taste. Cover with the lid and simmer gently on the top of the stove (do not boil) until done. Domestic rabbit will take 1½-2 hours; wild rabbit will take 2-2½ hours.

To make the dumplings, sift the flour and salt into a bowl and stir in the suet and parsley. Add enough of the cold water to bind to a

soft dough. Shape into large walnut-sized balls without
overhandling the dough.

Sometimes we make thyme dumpling using 4 sprigs of fresh
thyme. Make sure to strip the stems well and use only the
leaves as the little twigs can be unpleasant to chew. If fresh
thyme is not available, use 5 ml/1 tsp of dried.

About 30 minutes before the rabbit is ready, add the
dumplings, placing them on the surface of the stew. Cover
again and cook for 15 minutes then turn the dumplings over,
and add the peas and the mushrooms cut in half. Cook for a
further 15 minutes.

Adjust the seasoning before serving.

# HARE

In France, the regions produce differing species of hare and each acclaim the virtues of their variety. In Britain there are but two, the brown hare, similar to the Normandy hare, and the mountain hare, which is called the blue hare in Scotland. The American jackrabbit, which is really a hare, has white meat, whereas European species have dark meat.

The brown hare is larger than the mountain hare and it is more tender with a better flavour.

Young hares, which are called leverets, are very tender and, unlike mature hares, do not need to be marinated.

Hare is similar to wild rabbit with its fine-grained meat, but has a stronger flavour. When hare is shot it is usually hung head down and its blood collected; this is frequently used to thicken and enrich the cooking sauce. When the hare is bought from a supermarket, or when bought frozen, it is often difficult to obtain the blood. However frozen hare is available all year round.

Like many of the strong-flavoured game meats, hare is excellent in a sauce for Italian pasta.

The smell of hare cooking is very strong, so it is a good idea to cook a dish of hare the day before a dinner party and then to reheat it when ready to serve.

# Jugged Hare
### Serves 5 – 6

| METRIC/IMPERIAL | U.S. |
|---|---|
| 1 hare | 1 |
| 50 g/2 oz butter/vegetable margarine | 4 tbsp |
| 15 ml/1 tbsp sunflower oil | 1 tbsp |
| 3 medium onions | 3 |
| 3 carrots | 3 |
| 300 ml/½ pint stock | 1¼ cups |
| fine sea salt and freshly ground black pepper | |
| 30 ml/2 tbsp redcurrant jelly | 2 tbsp |
| 1 wineglass port wine | 1 wineglass |
| the blood of the hare or beurre manié to thicken | |
| MARINADE | |
| 600 ml/1 pint red wine | 2½ cups |
| 3 cloves | 3 |
| 2 pieces of lemon rind | 2 |
| freshly grated nutmeg | |
| 1 bay leaf | 1 |

Cut the hare into small joints. Marinate overnight in the red wine, cloves, lemon rind, nutmeg and bay leaf and turn the pieces occasionally in the marinade.

Preheat the oven to 170°C/325°F/Mark 3.

Remove the hare from the marinade and pat dry; reserve the marinade. Heat the butter and oil in a flameproof casserole.

Add the hare pieces and brown. Remove and keep warm. Add the onions and carrots, which you have sliced, and fry until brown. Remove and keep with the hare. Pour off any excess of fat from the casserole and put back the hare and the vegetables. Pour over the marinade and the stock. Season to taste with salt and pepper. Bring to the boil, then cover tightly and cook in the oven for 2-2½ hours or until the hare is tender.

Remove the hare to a hot serving dish. Strain the sauce into a saucepan and mix in the redcurrant jelly and port. Simmer for a few minutes, stirring well.

To thicken the sauce, gently heat the blood from the hare and add it slowly, stirring well. Do not allow to boil or the sauce will curdle. Taste for seasoning. If the blood is unavailable, thicken with beurre manié by mixing 25 g/1 oz flour into the 40 g/1½ oz

softened butter and whisking a little at a time into the sauce.
Pour the sauce over the hare and serve.

# Roast marinated saddle of hare
(Râble de lièvre)
Serves 2-3

| METRIC/IMPERIAL | U.S. |
|---|---|
| 1 saddle of hare | 1 |
| 40 g/1½ oz butter/vegetable margarine | 3 tbsp |
| fine sea salt and freshly ground black pepper | |
| 150 ml/¼ pint sour or single (light) cream | ⅔ cup |
| MARINADE | |
| 30 ml/2 tbsp olive oil | 2 tbsp |
| 15 ml/1 tbsp brandy | 1 tbsp |
| 150 ml/¼ pint red wine | ⅔ cup |
| 15 ml/1 tbsp wine vinegar | 1 tbsp |
| 1 shallot | 1 |
| 2 sprigs of thyme | 2 |
| 2 sprigs of parsley | 2 |

Combine the marinade ingredients. Add the saddle of hare and
leave to marinate overnight.
Preheat the oven to 189°C/350°F/Mark 4.
Remove the saddle of hare from the marinade and pat dry. Strain
the marinade and put on one side for later use. Melt the butter in
a small roasting pan. Put in the hare and baste with the butter.
Season with salt and pepper. Roast, basting frequently, for about
45 minutes. When cooked, remove from the pan and keep warm.
To make the sauce, deglaze the roasting pan with some of the
strained marinade. Pour into a small saucepan and add the
remaining marinade. Boil fast to reduce to half the quantity. Add
the sour cream or cream, heat without boiling and taste for
seasoning. Serve the saddle surrounded by Pears in Red Wine and
Brandy, page 112, with the sauce served separately.

# Casserole of hare provencal
(Civet de lièvre provencal)
Serves 4-5

| METRIC/IMPERIAL | U.S. |
|---|---|
| 1 hare | 1 |
| 4 rashers streaky (fatty) bacon | 6 slices |
| 2 cloves of garlic | 2 |
| 37.5 ml/2½ tbsp olive oil | 2½ tbsp |
| flour for coating | |
| 10-20 ml/2-4 tsp tomato paste | 2-4 tsp |
| 150 ml/¼ pint good stock | ¾ cup |
| freshly chopped parsley, chives and thyme, to garnish | |
| MARINADE | |
| 2 medium onions | 2 |
| 2 bay leaves | 2 |
| 2 each sprigs of thyme, sage and savory | 2 each |
| 1 clove of garlic | 1 |
| 6 black peppercorns | 6 |
| 450 ml/¾ pint red wine | 2 cups |
| 37.5 ml/2½ tbsp olive oil | 2½ tbsp |

Make a marinade of the finely sliced onions, bay leaves, herb sprigs, chopped garlic, peppercorns, red wine and oil. Mix well. Cut the hare into joints, place in the marinade and leave overnight.
Preheat the oven to 170°C/325°F/Mark 3.
Dice the bacon, and chop the garlic. Heat the oil in a flameproof casserole, add the bacon and garlic and brown. Remove and reserve. Drain the hare pieces and pat them dry; reserve the marinade. Add the hare to the casserole, sprinkle with flour and brown well. Replace the bacon and garlic. Add the marinade, tomato paste and enough stock to cover. Bring to the boil, then cover with foil and the lid and cook in the oven for 1½-2 hours or until the hare is tender. The sauce should be fairly thick.
Sprinkle the chopped herbs over before serving.

# Wide ribbon pasta with hare sauce

(Pappardelle con la lepre)
Serves 4

| METRIC/IMPERIAL | U.S. |
|---|---|
| 30 ml/2 tbsp olive oil | 2 tbsp |
| 50 g/2 oz butter/vegetable margarine | 4 tbsp |
| 50 g/2 oz lean bacon | 2 oz |
| 1 small onion | 1 |
| 1 stalk of celery | 1 |
| 600 g/1¼ lb meat cut from a hare | 1¼ lb |
| 5 ml/1 tsp dried thyme | 1 tsp |
| fine sea salt and freshly ground black pepper | |
| 15 ml/1 tbsp flour | 1 tbsp |
| 1 wineglass white wine | 1 wineglass |
| 500 ml/16 fl oz concentrated stock | 2 cups |
| 450 g/1 lb pappardelle or tagliatelle | 1 lb |
| freshly grated Parmesan cheese, to serve | |

A Tuscan recipe from Diane Seed's 'The Top 100 Pasta Sauces.'

Heat the oil and butter in a pan and gently fry the finely chopped bacon, onion and celery. Add the hare meat, cut into very small cubes, and the thyme and season to taste with salt and pepper. When the meat is browned, sprinkle with the flour; stir and brown the flour.
Add the wine and when that has almost evaporated add the boiling stock. Cover and cook gently for 2 hours.
Cook the pasta, following packet directions carefully to avoid overcooking. Drain and turn into a hot serving bowl. Stir in the sauce. Grated Parmesan cheese should be served separately.

# German Hare Casserole

(Geschmorter Hasenrücken)

Serves 2-3

| METRIC/IMPERIAL | U.S. |
|---|---|
| 1 saddle of hare | 1 |
| oil for frying | |
| 125 ml/4 fl oz meat stock | ½ cup |
| 1 shallot | 1 |
| 200 g/7 oz cooked peeled beetroot (beets) | 7 oz |
| 15 ml/1 tbsp fruit vinegar | 1 tbsp |
| 2.5 ml/½ tsp prepared mustard | ½ tsp |
| 30 ml/2 tbsp double cream (heavy cream) | 2 tbsp |
| fine sea salt and freshly ground black pepper | |
| 15 ml/1 tbsp wine vinegar | 1 tbsp |
| 30 ml/2 tbsp sour cream | 2 tbsp |
| MARINADE | |
| 600 ml/1 pint red wine | 2½ cups |
| 1 carrot | 1 |
| 1 onion | 1 |
| 1 bouquet garni comprising 3 sprigs of parsley, | 1 |
|     1 bay leaf, 1 small piece of orange peel and a little | |
|     basil and majoram | |
| 4 juniper berries | 4 |
| 5 ml/1 tsp oil | 1 tsp |

This German recipe is cooked in a *Römertopf*, a casserole rather like a chicken brick, which must be soaked in water for at least 15 minutes before use in an oven. It steams and bakes with very tender results.

Prepare the marinade by mixing together the carrot and onion, which you have chopped, the bouquet garni, juniper berries and oil. Put the hare into the marinade and leave for a good 24 hours. Preheat the oven to 220°C/425°F/Mark 7.
Pat the meat dry, (putting the marinade on one side), and fry quickly on all sides in heated oil. Place the hare in the well-soaked *Römertopf*. Pour on the strained marinade, meat stock and chopped shallot, cover and cook in the oven for about 1½ hours. Just before the hare is ready, cut the beetroot into thin slices and warm through in a pan.

Remove the hare and keep warm. Add the fruit vinegar, the mustard and cream to the sauce, with salt and pepper to taste. Pour in the rest of the vinegar, then mix in the sour cream. Carve the hare into slices, and serve sauce and beetroot separately.

# Hare in brown ale
### Serves 5–6

| METRIC/IMPERIAL | U.S. |
|---|---|
| 1 hare | 1 |
| flour for coating | |
| fine sea salt and freshly ground black pepper | |
| 15 g/½ oz butter | 1 tbsp |
| 300 ml/½ pint stock | 1¼ cups |
| 5 ml/1 tsp wine vinegar | 1 tsp |
| 6 cloves | 6 |
| 700 g/1½ lb potatoes, optional | 1½ lb |
| MARINADE | |
| 600 ml/1 pint brown ale (dark beer) | 2½ cups |
| 1 bay leaf | 1 |
| 1 clove of garlic | 1 |
| 3 large onions | 3 |

Make the marinade by mixing the beer, bay leaf, crushed garlic and sliced onions in a bowl. Cut the hare into joints, place in the marinade, and leave overnight.
Preheat the oven to 180°C/350°F/Mark 4.
Remove the hare from the marinade and pat dry. Coat with flour seasoned with salt and pepper. Heat the butter in a flameproof casserole. Add the hare and brown well. Add the marinade (unstrained), the stock, vinegar and cloves and bring to the boil. Cover with foil and lid and transfer to the oven. Cook for 1½-2 hours or until the hare is tender.
Taste for seasoning before serving.
If liked, slices of potato, dotted with butter, can be arranged on top of the hare for the last 45 minutes of cooking.

# PHEASANT

The pheasant is a Middle Eastern bird, named from the river Phasis and introduced to western Europe by the ancient Greeks and Romans. Somehow, it still inspires cooks to exotic variations.

Autumn is the best time to eat fresh pheasant. It is perhaps the most readily available of game birds, particularly as there are game farms that are rearing pheasant. Also many chicken recipes can be adapted to pheasant so it is not difficult for those who have not cooked game before. Having said that, there are a number of points worth remembering.

You will often be able to buy a brace of pheasant — a cock and hen together. The hen is more tender and has a better flavour.

Young birds are better for roasting; indeed, older birds can be incredibly tough, their sinewy legs being virtually inedible. In some supermarkets it is possible to buy pheasant with the entire legs removed.

How do you know it is a young bird? Generally, you can't always be sure. It is said that young cock pheasants will have shortish, round-ended spurs and that the wing tip feathers are more pointed than those on older birds, but if you buy from the supermarket the bird will be oven-ready with feet and feathers missing, though usually labelled as to suitability.

Many pheasants have deposits of deep yellow fat under their skin — perhaps from eating corn. This fat, with the skin, can be removed if you wish but you would then need to take other steps, such as covering with breadcrumbs, bacon, butter to prevent the bird from becoming too dry.

Pheasants vary considerably in size but a medium-sized bird should serve 2-4 people.

We have omitted the livers from most recipes, as they seem to be very difficult to obtain.

# Pheasant with foie gras and truffles
### (Faisan Souvaroff)
### Serves 2-3

| METRIC/IMPERIAL | U.S. |
|---|---|
| 1 good-sized undamaged hen pheasant | 1 |
| 1 small can of truffles or, preferably, 1 fresh truffle | 1 |
| 25 g/1 oz butter/vegetable margarine | 2 tbsp |
| 45 ml/3 tbsp foie gras or good quality chicken liver pâté | 3 tbsp |
| 125 ml/4 fl oz port wine | ½ cup |
| 125 ml/4 fl oz brandy | ½ cup |
| 125 ml/4 fl oz good chicken stock | ½ cup |
| fine sea salt and freshly ground black pepper | |
| flour and water paste, to seal | |

This is a most wonderful dish, to be shared only with those you love, on an extravagant occasion. We first ate it many years ago in the Dordogne region of France when it was made with chicken, but we have found it works even better with pheasant.

The day before, remove any unplucked feathers from the pheasant using tweezers. Wipe clean the pheasant and dry well. Cut the truffles into fine slices. With your fingers gently ease the skin away from the breast on the pheasant and slide in a few slices of truffle. Make a short cut in the legs; again gently easy away the skin and slide in a slice of truffle. If you have any truffle left, keep it with the juices from the can (you can keep this in the refrigerator for a week). We always use up all the truffle – this is not a dish to economise on. Truss the bird and keep in the refrigerator until ready to cook.

Preheat the oven to 180°C/350°F/Mark 4.

Heat the butter in a frying pan and brown the bird, taking care not to disturb the truffle slices. Transfer it to a cocotte or deep casserole. Cover the breast with foie gras or pâté and place the rest at the sides. Pour over the port, brandy, chicken stock, any remaining pieces of truffle and any truffle juices and season to taste with salt and pepper.

Make a flour and water paste and use to seal the casserole. Cook in the oven for 1-1½ hours.

When the pheasant is ready, everyone should be seated waiting. Unseal the casserole at the table. Although the paste breaks up and can make a mess on the tablecloth, the aroma that wafts out is something to be remembered for life.

# Pheasant casserole
## (Faisan bonne femme)
### Serves 4

| METRIC/IMPERIAL | U.S. |
|---|---|
| 2 small hen pheasants, or 1 large cock pheasant | 2 |
| 2 cloves of garlic | 2 |
| 10 ml/2 tsp dried thyme | 2 tsp |
| 90 g/3 ½ oz butter/ vegetable margarine | 7 tbsp |
| 30 ml/2 tbsp corn oil | 2 tbsp |
| 175 g/6 oz streaky (fatty) bacon | 6 oz |
| 4 medium carrotts | 4 |
| 4 medium potatoes | 4 |
| 12 small onions or shallots | 12 |
| fine sea salt and freshly ground black pepper | |
| 1 bouquet garni comprising parsley sprigs, 1 stalk of celery and 1 bay leaf | 1 |
| 1 wineglass Noilly Prat or other dry vermouth | 1 wineglass |

Preheat the oven to 180°C/350°F/Mark 4.
Wipe clean and dry the pheasants. Tidy them up by plucking out any remaining feathers. Chop the garlic and cream this with the thyme and butter. Place some of this mixture into the cavity of each bird and truss them. Brown the birds in the oil, then place them in a casserole.
Dice the bacon and brown it in the oil till the fat runs. Add the bacon to the casserole. Cut the carrots and potatoes into chunks about 2.5 cm/1 inch. These and the onions can be sautéed in oil if you wish, but we find this tends to make them too greasy so we put them straight into the casserole. If you wish to extend this dish simply add more vegetables and bacon. Season well, add the bouquet garni and the remaining garlic butter and pour on the Noilly Prat (an extra slug if you have extended the vegetables), Cover the casserole with a sheet of foil to make the lid fit more tightly, and cook for 1-½ hours, basting from time to time.

# Pheasant 'Ajja
### Serves 4

| METRIC/IMPERIAL | U.S. |
|---|---|
| 6 small shallots | 6 |
| corn or olive oil | |
| 40g/1½ oz pine nuts, optional | 3 tbsp |
| 40g/1½ oz sultanas (golden raisins), optional | 3 tbsp |
| 8-10 eggs | 8-10 |
| 450-700g/1-1½ lb cold meat from a cooked pheasant | 1-1½ lb |
| good bunch of parsley or coriander leaves (cilantro) | |
| 7½-10 ml/1½-2 tsp ground cinnamon | 1½-2 tsp |
| fine sea salt and freshly ground black pepper | |

This versatile recipe is a variation of a Middle Eastern dish which we have found invaluable for many occasions. It is misleading to call this dish an omelette, although under different names — Ij-jit, eggah — it is often referred to as such. 'Ajja are made with almost any vegetable, or mixture of vegetables, with added meat, fowl or game. The principal ingredient is eggs, which binds all the other ingredients together. An 'ajja is really like a very thick egg cake, and we often eat it lukewarm (the usual Arabic way of eating food) or cold — when it can be a very good first course for a rather grand picnic. It can be served with salad as a light lunch or in French bread as a sandwich.

Chop the shallots finely and cook in a little oil until translucent. Add the pine nuts and sultanas, if used, and cook for a few minutes.
Beat the eggs lightly in a large bowl. Add the fried mixture, the pheasant meat cut into small pieces, the chopped herbs, and cinnamon, salt and pepper to taste and stir. In a large heavy frying pan, heat some oil. Pour in the egg mixture, cover with the lid of the pan or with a plate and cook on a low heat for 15 minutes. Turn the 'ajja and cook on the other side for 10 minutes more — the contents of the pan must be firm and solid. To turn, invert the 'ajja on to another plate and slide back into the pan. Give extra cooking time if necessary — the surfaces must be well browned.

# Pheasant with apples and Calvados

(Faisan normand)

Serves 4

| METRIC/IMPERIAL | U.S. |
|---|---|
| 2 young plump pheasants | 2 |
| 4 large cooking (tart) apples | 4 |
| 40 g/1½ oz butter/vegetable margarine | 3 tbsp |
| 30 ml/2 tbsp corn or sunflower oil | 2 tbsp |
| 1½ wineglasses Calvados | 1½ wineglasses |
| 150 ml/¼ pint stock | ⅓ cup |
| fine sea salt and freshly ground black pepper | |
| icing (confectioners') sugar | |
| 300 ml/½ pint single (light) or double | |
| double (heavy) cream | 1¼ cups |

There are many variations of this wonderful combination of flavours and tastes. The pheasant can be cooked whole or jointed. The apples can be cooked in with the pheasant or added later. Whatever the variation you follow, the main ingredients are always: pheasant, apples, Calvados and fresh cream. We have tried many different versions, and the following is our favourite for this delicious warming winter dish.

Preheat the oven to 180°C/350°F/Mark 4.

Cut each pheasant into six pieces (as a chicken is jointed) or leave whole. Peel, core and slice two of the apples. Heat 15g/½oz (1 tbsp) of the butter with the oil in a heavy frying pan and brown the pheasant joints; remove. Sauté the sliced apples in the pan until tender.

Place the sliced apples in a flame-proof casserole and arrange the pheasants on top. Pour over the Calvados, stock and any juices left in the pan and season well with salt and pepper. Bring to the boil, cover and cook in the oven for 30-40 minutes.

Peel and core the remaining two apples and cut into rings. Sauté them in the remaining butter and sprinkle with sugar to caramelise.

Remove the pheasants to a hot serving dish. Reduce the sauce a little, then add the cream and heat gently — do not let the sauce boil if single (light) cream is used. Pour the sauce over the pheasant pieces or serve it separately (cut the pheasant in half if it was cooked whole). Garnish with the apple rings.

# Pheasant with cabbage
(Faisan rustique aux choux)
Serves 4

| METRIC/IMPERIAL | U.S. |
| --- | --- |
| 1 pheasant | 1 |
| 25 g/1 oz butter/vegetable margarine | 2 tbsp |
| 3 large onions | 3 |
| fine sea salt and freshly ground black pepper | |
| 2 large green cabbages | 2 |
| 4 small sausages | 4 |
| 1 ham knuckle (hock) | 1 |
| 1 bouquet garni comprising bay leaf, thyme and rosemary | |
| pinch of quatre-épices | |
| freshly chopped parsley, to garnish | |

A traditional French country recipe, kindly given to us by Julien, chef of "La Chaumière", a delightful small restaurant in Lauris-sur-Durance, in Provence. This simple and delicious method can also be used for partridge, but reduce the cooking time by about one third.

Wipe clean and dry the pheasant. Pluck out any remaining feathers, then truss the bird. Melt the butter in a large flameproof casserole and cook the pheasant over a hot flame until all sides are golden. Add the chopped onions, stir and add salt and pepper to taste. Cover with the lid and leave to cook over a very gentle heat for 1 hour.

During this time, wash and chop the cabbages, then blanch them in boiling salted water for 2 – 3 minutes. Drain the cabbage and add to the pheasant, with the sausages, ham, bouquet garni and spice. Allow them all to simmer for about 4 hours.

At the end of this time, remove the bouquet garni.

Untruss the pheasant and serve with the sausages and ham on a large dish, on top of a bed of cabbage, garnished with parsley.

# Roast Pheasant
### Serves 4

| METRIC/IMPERIAL | U.S. |
|---|---|
| 2 hen pheasants | 2 |
| 2 Petit Suisse or other soft low-fat cheeses | 2 |
| 22 ml/1½ tbsp softened butter/ | |
|     vegetable margarine | 1½ tbsp |
| streaky (fatty) bacon, optional | |
| 3-4 juniper berries | 3-4 |
| 1 wineglass Madeira | 1 wineglass |
| 300 ml/½ pint good chicken stock | 1¼ cups |
| fine sea salt and freshly ground black pepper. | |

A simple way to roast pheasant, as easy as roasting chicken, and a welcome change.

Pre-heat the oven to 190°C/375°F/Mark 5.
Wipe clean and dry the birds well. Check that there are no feathers left unplucked. Place a Petit Suisse cheese in the cavity of each pheasant. Truss, and rub them thoroughly with softened butter. Cover the breasts with bacon. The bacon stops the birds from drying out; if you prefer, use foil as a covering.
Stand the birds on a trivet in a small roasting pan. Add the crushed juniper berries, the Madeira and stock to the pan. Roast for 45-55 minutes. Baste from time to time with the juices in the pan. Remove the bacon or foil covering 10 minutes before the end of the cooking time to allow the breasts to brown.
Untruss the pheasants, season well, and serve with the pan juices reduced as a sauce.

# PIGEON

Wild wood pigeons are at their best in the spring and summer months. This is the time when they infuriate the farmers by scoffing their crops of cabbages and corn.

Young birds (squabs), which are usually bred for the table, have rounder breasts and softer, pinker legs and are best for roasting. Alas, these can be hard to find fresh, but are available frozen the year around in the United States. These delicate young birds are ideal for recipes like the Salade Tiède on page 41.

Older birds, more commonly available, are best casseroled or pot-roasted or made into game pies, or dishes such as the pigeon, hare and ham terrine on page 104.

Pigeon freezes well, especially if frozen during the summer months, and it is now commonly available frozen from supermarkets, plucked and trussed ready for cooking.

Allow one bird per person. Sometimes, when only the breast is being used, more than one bird per person will be needed.

# Pigeon with 40 cloves of garlic
### Serves 4

| METRIC/IMPERIAL | U.S. |
|---|---|
| 125-175 ml/4-6 fl oz good olive oil | ½-¾ cup |
| 4 pigeons | 4 |
| 40 cloves garlic | 40 |
| 2 stalks young celery | 2 |
| 4 sprigs parsley | 4 |
| 4 sprigs thyme, preferably lemon thyme | 4 |
| 1 sprig rosemary | 1 |
| 1 bay leaf | 1 |
| fine sea salt and freshly ground black pepper | |

This is an adaptation of a marvellous chicken recipe we often served to friends in the South of France. There you can get those fat, pink heads of Provencal garlic which is much milder than many other strains. But you still need to be a lover of this invaluable and healthy herb to enjoy the dish. One day we were given four pigeons, so we decided to try them instead – it worked splendidly.

Preheat the oven to 180°C/350°F/Mark 4.
Pour the olive oil into a casserole. Put in the pigeons and roll them over so that they become well covered in oil. Add all those delicious cloves of garlic, in their skins, the celery, herbs and salt and pepper to taste. Cover the casserole and seal closely with foil or with a flour and water paste.
Cook for 1½-2 hours. At the end of this time, the pigeons will be tender, the garlic soft and your friends, driven mad by the aroma, will be anxious to eat. Serve immediately with lots of French bread to mop up the juice.
As the garlic cloves will still be in their skins you may need a little practice in removing them. Hold one end with your fork, squeeze gently along the clove with your knife blade and out will come the soft and delicate centre.

# Warm pigeon salad with quail's eggs

(Salade tiède de pigeon)
Serves 4

| METRIC/IMPERIAL | U.S. |
|---|---|
| 100 g/4 oz fine green beans | ¼ lb |
| 2 medium tomatoes | 2 |
| salad leaves including raddichio, endive (chicory) and lamb's lettuce (corn salad) | |
| the breasts of 2 pigeons, skinned and lightly beaten | |
| grapeseed oil | |
| 4 quail's eggs | 4 |
| vinaigrette, made with olive oil, lemon juice, Dijon mustard, fine sea salt and freshly ground black pepper | |

This is a very light and pretty salad which we have made many times, sometimes using pigeon and sometimes, if young pigeon is not available using quail breasts.

Blanch the beans in boiling salted water for about 2 minutes. Drain and refresh in cold water. Drain again and dry well. Skin the tomatoes by putting them in a bowl, pouring boiling water over them, counting 12 and then plunging them into cold water. The skins come off quite easily after this treatment. Thinly slice the tomatoes.
Make up the plates by first arranging the salad leaves into a nest shape on each. Put a couple of thin slices of tomato into each nest. Cut the beans into 2.5 cm/1 inch pieces and put on top of the tomatoes.
Now you will need to do two things at the same time. Sauté the pigeon breasts in grapeseed oil till brown on both sides but still pink on the inside. In a second pan fry the quail's eggs – also in grapeseed oil – keeping the yolks soft.
With a very sharp knife, quickly slice each breast piece into 3–4 slices and lay them on the beans. Place the eggs on top of the pigeon slices. Dress the salads with the pan sauces and a not too sharp vinaigrette. Serve immediately.

# Julia's pigeon
Serves 4

| METRIC/IMPERIAL | U.S. |
|---|---|
| 16 pitted prunes | 16 |
| 2 wineglasses port wine | 2 wineglasses |
| 25 g/1 oz butter/vegetable margarine | 2 tbsp |
| sunflower oil | |
| flour for coating | |
| 4 pigeons | 4 |
| fine sea salt and freshly ground black pepper | |
| 4 Petit Suisse or other soft low-fat cheeses | 4 |
| 150 ml/¼ pint chicken stock | ⅔ cup |
| 4 medium leeks | 4 |
| 8 juniper berries | 8 |
| lemon juice, to taste | |

There are many pigeon recipes using grapes with Madeira, but other fruit and wine combinations can be just as successful. One day, Edward's daughter, Julia, was bringing her family to lunch, and knowing her fondness for prunes we decided to cook the pigeon with prunes and port instead of the more usual grapes and Madeira. It was delicious.

Soak the prunes overnight in half of the port.
Preheat the oven to 180°C/350°F/Mark 4.
Heat the butter with a little oil in a flameproof casserole. Flour the pigeons and brown them carefully all over. Season the cavities of the birds, and place a Petit Suisse cheese inside each one. Add the prunes, all of the port, stock and seasoning to the casserole. Cut the leeks into 2.5 cm/1 inch pieces, crush the juniper berries and add these to the casserole. Bring to the boil, then seal with a cover of foil under the lid.
Cook in the oven for 1½-2 hours.
Before serving, taste for seasoning and, if the sauce is a little too sweet for your taste, add some lemon juice.

# Pigeon with green peas
Serves 4

| METRIC/IMPERIAL | U.S. |
|---|---|
| 4 pigeons | 4 |
| 2.5 ml/½ tsp ground allspice | ½ tsp |
| fine sea salt and freshly ground black pepper | |
| 8 rashers streaky (fatty) bacon | 8 slices |
| 50 g/2 oz melted butter/vegetable margarine | 4 tbsp |
| 300 ml/½ pint chicken stock | 1¼ cups |
| 1 small, tender lettuce | 1 |
| 10 spring onions (scallions) | 10 |
| 350 g/12 oz shelled fresh peas | 2 ⅓ cups |
| 7.5 ml/1½ tsp brown sugar | 1½ tsp |
| beurre manié to thicken, optional | |

Preheat the oven to 180°C/350°F/Mark 4.
Place the pigeons in a flameproof casserole. Season to taste with allspice, salt and pepper, and cover with the bacon. Pour over half of the melted butter and the chicken stock and bring to the boil. Cover and cook in the oven for 1½-2 hours. Baste the birds often. About 20 minutes before the pigeons are ready, remove the lid and bacon to allow the breasts to brown.
About 45 minutes before the pigeons are cooked, place about half of the remaining butter in another casserole and cover the bottom with a layer of half of the shredded lettuce leaves. Cut the spring onions (scallions) in 1 cm/½ inch pieces and add them to the casserole together with the peas, brown sugar and salt and pepper to taste. Lay the remainder of the shredded lettuce on top and pour over the last of the butter. Cover firmly with the lid and put in the oven beside the other casserole. The peas will take about 30 minutes to cook. When ready, the onions and lettuce should be a little crunchy.
When cooked remove the casserole with the pigeons. Take them out and keep warm. (We like to eat the bacon so we also keep that warm with the pigeons.) Skim off any fat you do not want on the sauce and adjust for seasoning. If you wish, you can thicken the sauce with beurre manié. (see page 24).
Put the green pea mixture on to a hot serving dish and sit the pigeons, together with the bacon, on top.
Serve the sauce separately.

# Roast pigeons on chicken liver canapés
(Pigeons sur canapés)
Serves 4

| METRIC/IMPERIAL | U.S. |
|---|---|
| 4 young pigeons | 4 |
| flour for coating | |
| 2 sprigs of French tarragon | 2 |
| fine sea salt and freshly ground black pepper | |
| 90 g/3½ oz butter/vegetable margarine | 7 tbsp |
| 8 rashers streaky (fatty) bacon | 8 slices |
| 90 ml/6 tbsp sunflower or grapeseed oil | 6 tbsp |
| 450 g/1 lb white mushrooms | 1 lb |
| 1 clove of garlic | 1 |
| 4 slices of wholemeal (whole wheat) or white bread | 4 |
| 8 chicken livers | 8 |
| 125 ml/4 fl oz port wine or Madeira | ½ cup |
| 37.5 ml/2½ tbsp chopped spring onions (scallions) | 2½ tbsp |
| 300 ml/½ pint chicken stock | 1¼ cups |
| freshly chopped parsley or watercress to garnish | |

This is a variation of a classic but simple French recipe which should only be made if you are sure you have young tender pigeons.

Preheat the oven to 200°C/400°F/Mark 6.
Roll the birds in flour. Season the cavities with chopped tarragon, salt and pepper and add a tiny piece of butter. Cover the birds with the bacon. Place the pigeons on a trivet in a shallow roasting pan, add a little butter and oil to the pan and roast for 25-30 minutes. Baste the birds frequently.
Meanwhile, quarter the mushrooms if they are large, and sauté them in a mixture of butter and oil for about 4 minutes. Add the crushed garlic, simmer for 1 minute and remove from the heat. Keep warm.
Remove the crusts and fry the bread in oil and reserve.
Trim the livers and mash them in a small bowl with 15 ml/1 tbsp of the port or Madeira and salt and pepper to taste. Spread this mixture on to the slices of fried bread and reserve.
When the pigeons are cooked, take them from the roasting pan and keep warm. To make the sauce, remove all but 22 ml/1½ tbsp of the fat from the roasting pan and stir in the chopped spring

44

onions (scallions). Sauté until softened, then add the stock and the remaining port or Madeira. Make sure you scrape the sides and bottom of the dish well to incorporate the sediment. Boil briskly until reduced by one-third.

Check that the mushrooms are still hot. Put the liver canapés under a very hot grill (broiler) for 1-2 minutes to cook the mixture, but make sure they don't burn. Arrange them on a hot dish and place a pigeon on each surrounded by the mushrooms. Garnish with herbs and serve with the sauce.

# Pigeon pot-roasted in vermouth

(Pigeon en cocotte)

Serves 4

| METRIC/IMPERIAL | U.S. |
|---|---|
| 30 ml/2 tbsp sunflower oil | 2 tbsp |
| 25 g/1 oz butter/vegetable margarine | 2 tbsp |
| flour for coating | |
| 4 pigeons | 4 |
| 18 shallots or button (pearl) onions | 18 |
| 175 g/6 oz salt pork | 6 oz |
| 100 g/4 oz button mushrooms | ¼ lb |
| 150 ml/¼ pint dry vermouth or white wine | ⅔ cup |
| 150 ml/¼ pint chicken stock | ⅔ cup |
| fine sea salt and freshly gound black pepper | |
| freshly chopped mixed herbs such as parsley and chives. | |

Preheat the oven to 180°C/350°F/Mark 4.

Heat the oil and butter in a frying pan. Flour the pigeons and brown them carefully all over; remove. Put the onions in a saucepan of cold water, bring to the boil and simmer for 2 minutes, then drain well. Cut the pork into small cubes and sauté in the frying pan till the fat runs. Add the onions and mushrooms and brown. Tip the pork, onions and mushrooms into a strainer and drain off the fat.

Put the pigeons, pork, onions, mushrooms, vermouth, stock, and salt and pepper to taste in a cocotte or flameproof casserole. Bring to the boil, then cover with a double layer of foil and the lid to seal as tightly as possible and transfer to the oven. Cook for 1½-2 hours. Just before serving, sprinkle the chopped herbs over the contents of the cocotte.

# QUAIL

The common quail, once a migratory bird, is now bred in Europe for the table. Both it and its delightful little speckled eggs are increasingly available in the shops. The American quail, a slightly larger and very delicate bird, is a member of the American partridge family. It can be used in the recipes here or for partridge.

Quails are sometimes sold already boned, but it is better to bone them yourself — it is not difficult. Boned commercially, we have found, means that the birds often finish up looking rather messy, and with such a small bird, presentation is very important. If they are not boned you will need, as a main course, at least two birds per person. Boned and stuffed, one should be sufficient.

Quail are the most convenient of game birds. They are available all the year round, and being so small they are ideal fast food. Many years ago, Edouard de Pomiane, included sautéed quails in his famous 'Cooking in Ten Minutes', which was, perhaps, a little optimistic. But whether you roast, grill or casserole them they seldom need as much as 25 minutes, plus a few minutes for resting. If they are stuffed they may need to be cooked for a full half-hour.

# Grilled quail
### Serves 4

| METRIC/IMPERIAL | U.S. |
|---|---|
| 8 quail | 8 |
| lemon juice | |
| paprika, to garnish | |
| MARINADE | |
| 150 ml/¼ pint olive or sunflower oil | ⅔ cups |
| 2 cloves of garlic | 2 |
| 5 ml/1 tsp dried thyme | 1 tsp |
| 5 ml/1 tsp dried rosemary | 1 tsp |
| 5 ml/1 tsp dried savory | 1 tsp |
| 7.5 ml/1½ tsp finely crumbled dried bay leaf | 1½ tsp |
| 2.5 ml/½ tsp paprika | ½ tsp |
| fine sea salt and freshly ground black pepper | |

Quail are best grilled on a barbecue with generous handfuls of herbs thrown on to the embers. But if this is not practical, indoors will do, with the grill (broiler) switched on well in advance to make certain that it is really hot.

Split open the quail and, splay or spatchcock them. Mix together all the ingredients for the marinade in a flat dish, chopping the garlic roughly, and marinate the quail in this for about 5 hours or even overnight. Turn them from time to time so that they are well soaked in these sunshine herbs.

Grill (broil) the birds; this will take 8-12 minutes depending upon the heat. Baste them frequently with the marinade. When cooked, the skin should be brown but not charred. Serve immediately, with a squeeze of lemon and a sprinkle of paprika.

Pitta bread and a salad, made the Greek way with cucumber, tomatoes, black olives, feta cheese, a lot of olive oil and a sprinkle of parsley, go well with this.

# Sweet and sour quail
### Serves 4

| METRIC/IMPERIAL | U.S. |
|---|---|
| 8 quail | 8 |
| little oil for frying | |
| 4 stalks of celery | 4 |
| 4 medium carrots | 4 |
| 2 medium onions | 2 |
| 50 g/2 oz fine green beans | 2 oz |
| fine sea salt and freshly ground black pepper | |
| 45 ml/3 tbsp capers | 3 tbsp |
| 60-75 ml/4-5 tbsp olive or sunflower oil | 4-5 tbsp |
| 60-75 ml/4-5 tbsp white wine vinegar | 4-5 tbsp |
| 7.5 ml/1½ tsp sugar | 1½ tsp |
| bunch of parsley or few sprigs of coriander leaves (cilantro) | |

We saw this very pretty dish, or something very similar, being made for us through the glass partition that separated dining room from kitchen in a splendid restaurant overlooking Lake Maggiore. We experimented to reproduce this sweet and sour quail as close to the original as possible.

Brown the quail in a little oil in a flameproof casserole or saucepan. Chop the celery; cut the carrots into thin rings; chop the onions into small dice; and cut the beans into 2.5.cm/1 inch pieces. Add the vegetables to the quail with salt and pepper to taste and just enough water to cover the birds. Cover with foil and the lid and bring to the boil, then simmer for 15-25 minutes or until cooked.
Remove the quail and place on a hot serving dish. Strain the cooking liquid into a small pan; arrange the vegetables around the quail. Boil to reduce the liquid a little, then add the capers, olive oil, vinegar and sugar and bring back to the boil.
Simmer for a few minutes.
Pour the sauce over the quail, or serve it separately, and scatter the chopped herbs on top.

# Roast quail with kiwi
### Serves 4

| METRIC/IMPERIAL | U.S. |
| --- | --- |
| 40 g/1½ oz butter/ vegetable margarine | 3 tbsp |
| 8 quail | 8 |
| 8 rashers streaky (fatty) bacon | 8 slices |
| 1-2 wineglasses dry white wine | 1-2 wineglasses |
| 4 kiwi fruit | 4 |
| 15 ml/1 tbsp brandy | 1 tbsp |
| fine sea salt and freshly ground black pepper | |

Preheat the oven to 180°C/350°F/Mark 4.
Rub the quail with butter or oil and wrap in the bacon. Arrange them in a buttered baking dish, just big enough to hold them. Add 1 wineglass of wine and roast for 20-25 minutes.
Peel and slice the kiwi into rounds. Wrap in foil and place in the oven for the last 4-5 minutes of cooking – just long enough to warm them through.
Remove the quail to a hot serving dish. Drain off most of the fat from the baking dish, and add the brandy with salt and pepper to taste. Flame it and extinguish by adding a little more wine. Scrape up the residue in the bottom of the dish and simmer for 1-2 minutes. Taste for seasoning.
Place the kiwi fruit around the quail and pour the sauce on top.

# Quail with ham and peas
### (Cailles à la romaine)

### Serves 4

| METRIC/IMPERIAL | U.S. |
| --- | --- |
| 30 ml/2 tbsp olive oil | 2 tbsp |
| 8 quail | 8 |
| 100 g/4 oz good Parma ham or lean cooked ham | ¼ lb |
| 2 medium onions | 2 |
| 350 g/12 oz fresh peas or frozen | 2⅓ cups |
| 300-450 ml/½-¾ pint ham or chicken stock | 1¼-2 cups |
| 7.5 ml/1½ tsp sugar | 1½ tsp |
| fine sea salt and freshly ground pepper | |

This is a very simple casserole dish with a lot of flavour. There are a number of alternative ingredients which make it easy to assemble. If using ham stock, taste it to be sure it isn't too salty.

Heat the oil in a flameproof casserole and brown the quail well. Dice the ham and add this, together with the finely chopped onions, peas, stock, sugar and salt and pepper to taste. Cover tightly with the lid and foil. Bring to the boil, then reduce to a simmer and cook for 15-25 minutes.
Serve direct from the casserole.

# Quail with thyme and shallots
Serves 4

| METRIC/IMPERIAL | U.S. |
|---|---|
| 60 ml/4 tbsp olive oil | ¼ cup |
| 8 quail | 8 |
| 16 shallots | 16 |
| 10 ml/2 tsp dried thyme | 2 tsp |
| 3 cloves of garlic | 3 |
| 300 ml/½ pint rosé wine | 1¼ cups |
| fine sea salt and freshly ground black pepper | |
| 150 ml/¼ pint chicken stock | ⅔ cup |

Heat the oil in a large, flameproof casserole. Add the quail and brown them well. Remove and keep warm. Gently sauté the finely sliced shallots until brown. Return the quail to the casserole and sprinkle them with the thyme and finely chopped garlic. Pour in the wine and add salt and pepper to taste. Bring to the boil, then cover with foil and the lid and simmer for 15-25 minutes or until done.
Remove the quail and keep hot. Add the chicken stock to the juices in the pan and boil briskly to reduce a little. Taste for seasoning.
Serve the quail on a hot serving dish with the sauce poured over them or served separately.

# GUINEA FOWL

Guinea fowl, originally an African bird, has been a delight in Europe from Roman times when it was known as the hen of Carthage. The birds were taken to North America by Europeans who regarded them as a great delicacy for special occasions.

Strictly guinea fowl is not classified as game, but as there are so many delightful recipes and as it is usually found on the game counter of the butcher or supermarket we have no hesitation in including it. Many regard it as a more interesting chicken, and indeed it can serve very well in classic chicken dishes such as *coq au vin*. Others find it has, in some respects, a similarity to pheasant — and again many of the recipes are interchangeable.

One advantage over pheasant is that the legs of the guinea fowl, having fewer tendons and sinews, are much more easily edible. As guinea fowl are not subject to game laws there is no closed hunting season, so it is possible — if you can find them — to buy them fresh all the year round.

# Curried guinea fowl
## Serves 4

| METRIC/IMPERIAL | U.S. |
|---|---|
| 3 stalks of celery | 3 |
| 1 large onion | 1 |
| ½ sweet red pepper | ½ |
| ½ sweet green pepper | ½ |
| 2 cloves of garlic | 2 |
| 30-45 ml/2-3 tbsp sunflower oil | 2-3 tbsp |
| seeds from 3 pods of green cardamom | |
| 10 ml/2 tsp turmeric | 2 tsp |
| 7.5 ml/1½ tsp ground cinnamon | 1½ tsp |
| 5 ml/1 tsp ground caraway | 1 tsp |
| 5 ml/1 tsp ground cumin | 1 tsp |
| 5 ml/1 tsp ground ginger | 1 tsp |
| 5 ml/1 tsp cayenne pepper | 1 tsp |
| 30 ml/2 tbsp tomato paste | 2 tbsp |
| 400 g/14 oz canned tomatoes | 14 oz |
| 150 ml/¼ pint chicken stock | ⅔ cup |
| fine sea salt and freshly ground black pepper | |
| 1 guinea fowl | 1 |
| 1 small ripe mango or | 1 |
| 15 ml/1 tbsp mango chutney | 1 tbsp |
| 50 g/2 oz sultanas (golden raisins) optional | 6 tbsp |

This lively and spicy recipe was made for us, using chicken, by Piers and Judith Bastard, two gentle but expert safari guides from Kenya. It can be made as hot as you wish and, we imagine, under a starlit African sky the stronger the better. But we always keep it mild, otherwise it overwhelms the guinea fowl. Judith always makes the sauce 1 or 2 days before it is required to allow the many flavours to amalgamate thoroughly. If possible freshly grind the cinnamon, caraway and cumin yourself, in a spice or coffee grinder. In any case, make sure you use spices which have not been kept in your storecupboard too long.

Chop the celery, onion, peppers and garlic and brown in a little of the oil. Add the crushed cardamon seeds with all the ground spices and brown with the vegetables. Stir in the tomato paste, tomatoes, stock, and salt and pepper to taste. The sauce should

be the consistency of a thick soup. Cool, then cover and leave
in the refrigerator until needed.
Cut the guinea fowl into joints and gently brown it in the
remaining oil. Put the pieces in a saucepan together with the
sauce. Chop the mango and add (or add the chutney) with the
sultanas. Cover and simmer for 40 minutes to 1 hour.
Taste the sauce. If you would like it to be hotter, gradually add
more cayenne pepper or ½-1 chopped hot green chilli. If you
want to make the sauce sweeter, add more mango chutney.

# Pot-roast of quinea fowl
Serves 4

| METRIC/IMPERIAL | U.S. |
|---|---|
| 1-2 guinea fowl, depending on size | 1-2 |
| 1 Spanish onion | 1 |
| 60 ml/4 tbsp olive oil | ¼ cup |
| 4 sprigs marjoram | 4 |
| 4 sprigs rosemary | 4 |
| 2 sprigs savory | 2 |
| 2 wineglasses dry white wine | 2 wineglasses |
| fine sea salt and freshly ground black pepper | |

One could hardly do better than have a guinea fowl, simply pot
roasted, scented with a few fresh herbs, and served with tiny new
scrubbed potatoes, sprinkled with black pepper and dill. In
Provence, we often ate it as an exciting alternative to chicken. If
fresh herbs are not available you can use 5 ml/1 tsp each dried
marjoram and rosemary, and 2.5 ml/½ tsp dried savory.

Preheat the oven to 180°C/350°F/Mark 4.
Clean and dry the quinea fowl well. If there are any stray feathers
tidy them away with a pair of tweezers. Stuff the cavity with the
onion cut into quarters, then truss the bird. Heat the oil to
smoking in a frying pan, add the guinea fowl and brown well.
In a casserole just big enough to hold the bird, make a bed of the
herbs and a little of the oil. Put in the bird and pour on the wine.
Season to taste with salt and pepper. Cover with the lid, bring to
the boil and cook in the oven for 45 minutes to 1 hour.
Remove the onion from the cavity before carving. Strain the
sauce and serve separately.

# Guinea fowl tagine
Serves 4

| METRIC/IMPERIAL | U.S. |
|---|---|
| 1 guinea fowl | 1 |
| 25 g/1 oz butter or | 2 tbsp |
| 30 ml/2 tbsp olive oil | 2 tbsp |
| 2.5 ml/½ tsp powdered saffron | ½ tsp |
| 1.25 ml/¼ tsp ground cumin | ¼ tsp |
| 1.25 ml/¼ tsp paprika | ¼ tsp |
| fine sea salt and freshly ground black pepper | |
| 225 g/8 oz Spanish onions | ½ lb |
| 50 g/2 oz canned chick peas (garbanzos) | ⅓ cup |
| 300-450 ml/½-¾ pint well-flavoured | |
| chicken stock | 1¼-2 cups |
| 50 g/2 oz blanched almonds | ⅓ cups |
| 25 g/1 oz sultanas (golden raisins) | 3 tbsp |
| 25 g/1 oz raisins | 3 tbsp |
| 1.25 ml/¼ tsp ground cinnamon | ¼ tsp |
| 225 g/8 oz Basmati rice | 1⅓ cups |
| freshly chopped parsley, to garnish | |

This is a very good-tempered dish and will stay happily simmering for an extra hour if necessary, but turned down very low. When ready the guinea fowl should be falling off the bones and the sauce well reduced. The dish is a most beautiful colour, particularly when sprinkled with parsley.

Cut the guinea fowl into joints. Sauté the pieces in some of the butter or oil with half the saffron, the cumin, paprika, and salt and pepper to taste until golden brown. In another pan, sauté half the onions until brown. Put the guinea fowl, spices and fried onions in a casserole with the chick peas and stock and simmer gently for about 45 minutes to 1 hour until tender.

Meanwhile, fry the rest of the onions in the remaining butter or oil until brown, then add the almonds, sultanas (golden raisins) and raisins. Sprinkle with cinnamon and put aside; keep warm.

Cook the rice with the remaining saffron and keep hot.

Serve the guinea fowl in its sauce and the rice separately, sprinkling the rice with the almond mixture, or serve the guinea fowl sitting on a bed of rice, sprinkled with the almond mixture, with the sauce separately.

# Guinea fowl with mushrooms and apricots

Serves 4

| METRIC/IMPERIAL | U.S. |
|---|---|
| 12 dried apricots | 12 |
| 1 guinea fowl | 1 |
| 15 g/½ oz butter/ vegetable margarine | 1 tbsp |
| 2 wineglasses dry white wine | 2 wineglasses |
| fine sea salt and freshly ground black pepper | |
| 350 g/12 oz large field mushrooms | ¾ lb |
| 1 clove of garlic | 1 |
| 30 ml/2 tbsp olive oil | 2 tbsp |
| freshly chopped parsley | |

Soak the apricots in warm water for about 3 hours or until they plump up. Drain.

Clean and dry the guinea fowl and truss it. Melt the butter in a flameproof casserole and brown the bird well. Add the apricots, white wine, and salt and pepper to taste. Simmer, with the lid on, over a moderate heat for about 45 minutes. Baste frequently.

Clean the mushrooms (wiping them with damp kitchen paper is usually sufficient). Chop the garlic. About 10 minutes before the guinea fowl is ready, cook the mushrooms in the olive oil — a cover on the pan will help to cook them without burning. Season and add the garlic and parsley.

You can either carve the guinea fowl or cut it into quarters. Place it on a hot serving dish and surround it with the apricots and sauce. Serve the mushrooms on the same dish or separately.

# PARTRIDGE

The best time for eating partridge is late autumn. Young partridges are tender and have a delicate flavour but older birds can be exceedingly tough. It is important, therefore, if you buy them frozen that they be labelled accurately stating whether they should be roasted or casseroled.

Two varieties are available — the red legged or French, which is the larger of the two, and the grey or English partridge, which has olive-coloured legs. The grey has probably the better flavour. There is no native American partridge, and, confusingly, the name is used for ruffed grouse in the north and for quail in the south. But both the true partridges are imported into the U.S.

It is usual to serve one partridge for each person, but if they are large birds they can be split in half. This, of course, reduces the cooking time.

If you can get the livers, always use them in your recipes, but we have found that with supermarket birds the liver has usually been removed.

# Grilled partridge
### Serves 4

| METRIC/IMPERIAL | U.S. |
|---|---|
| 4 young partridges | 4 |
| 45 ml/3 tbsp olive oil | 3 tbsp |
| 3.25 ml/¾ tsp ground coriander | ¾ tsp |
| 2.5 ml/½ tsp ground cumin | ½ tsp |
| fine sea salt and freshly ground black pepper | |

A simple dish very quicky prepared — but delicious.
The very first thing to do when grilling (broiling) any dish is to
turn on the grill (broiler) to high to make sure it is very, very hot.
Split the partridge open down the back — a large carving knife
pressed firmly down will do this — and splay or spatchcock them.
Make a sauce of the olive oil, spices and salt and pepper to taste.
Paint the birds all over very thoroughly with the mixture.
Grill (broil) them for 8-15 minutes, depending on the size birds
and the heat. Turn them frequently, and do not char the skin.
Place on hot plates, sprinkle with parsley and squeeze lemon juice
on them. Serve with a fresh tomato sauce.

# Roast partridge
## Serves 4

| METRIC/IMPERIAL | U.S. |
|---|---|
| 4 young partridges | a4 |
| 25 g/1 oz butter/vegetable margarine | 2 tbsp |
| 4 slices of fat bacon or pork fat | 4 |
| flour for dredging | |
| fine sea salt and freshly ground black pepper | |
| watercress, to garnish | |

This is the most common method of cooking partridge and perhaps the best — so long as the birds are young and tender.

Preheat the oven to 220°C/425°F/Mark 7.
Wipe clean and dry the partridges. Divide the butter into four pieces and place a piece inside the cavity of each bird. Truss them and cover the breasts with the bacon or pork fat. Place the birds on a trivet in a roasting pan. Roast for 25-40 minutes. Baste frequently.
A few minutes before the partridges are ready, remove the bacon. Dredge the breasts with flour and baste again. Continue to cook till the breasts are brown.
Remove the trussing strings and place on a very hot serving dish. Season with salt and pepper, garnish with watercress and serve.

# Partridge in a jacket of vine leaves
## Serves 4

| METRIC/IMPERIAL | U.S. |
|---|---|
| 4 young partridges | 4 |
| 75 g/3 oz softened butter/vegetable margarine | 6 tbsp |
| juice of ½ lemon | |
| 15 ml/3 tsp freshly chopped chives | 3 tsp |
| fine sea salt and freshly ground black pepper | |
| 4 slices of fat bacon or pork fat | 4 |
| 8-12 vine (grape) leaves, fresh if possible | 8-12 |
| 2 carrots | 2 |
| 2 parsnips | 2 |
| 1 wineglass dry white wine | 1 wineglass |
| flour for dredging | |

Preheat the oven to 200°C/400°F/Mark 6.

Wipe clean and dry the partridges thoroughly. Mix the butter with the lemon juice, chives, and salt and pepper to taste. Divide the mixture into four and place in the cavities of the birds. Truss them. Wrap the partridges in the bacon or pork fat and tie two or three vine (grape) leaves around each to form a jacket.

Cut the carrots and parsnips into thin rounds and make a layer in a small baking dish. Place the partridge on top and pour over the wine. Cook for 25-40 minutes. A few minutes before the partridges are ready, remove all the coverings, dredge with flour, baste and continue cooking till brown.

We like to serve the partridges on a bed of the vegetables. Use the crisp bacon, if you like to eat it, as a garnish.

# Partridge in peppers
### Serves 4

| METRIC/IMPERIAL | U.S. |
|---|---|
| 65 g/2½ oz butter/vegetable margarine | 5 tbsp |
| 30 ml/2 tbsp corn oil | 2 tbsp |
| 4 partridges | 4 |
| 1 medium onion | 1 |
| 2 cloves of garlic | 2 |
| 2 sweet red peppers, or 1 red and 1 yellow | 2 |
| 5 ml/1 tsp dried thyme | 1 tsp |
| fine sea salt and freshly ground black pepper | |
| 175 ml/6 fl oz dry white wine | ¾ cup |
| 175 ml/6 fl oz good chicken stock | ¾ cup |
| 25 g/1 oz flour | 3 tbsp |
| 90-120 ml/6-8 tbsp single (light) or double (heavy) cream, optional | 6-8 tbsp |

Heat the 25 g/1 oz of butter and the oil in a flameproof casserole. Brown the partridges and remove. Slice the onion thinly, and finely chop the garlic. Fry them in the casserole until translucent, then remove from the heat.

Remove the seeds and pith from the peppers and slice into julienne strips. Parboil them until slightly soft, then drain.

Put the partridges back into the casserole with the onion and garlic and add the strips of pepper, thyme, and salt and pepper to taste. Add the wine and chicken stock and bring to the boil. Cover the casserole with foil and the lid and reduce the heat until simmering. Cook for 35-45 minutes.

When done, remove the partridges to a hot serving dish. Strain the cooking liquid into a saucepan; arrange the vegetables on and around the partridges.

Bring the cooking liquid to simmer. Make a *beurre manié* with the remaining butter and the flour and add to the liquid, a small lump at a time, whisking until the sauce begins to thicken and shine. Remove from the heat and strain again if at all lumpy. Add the cream and heat again, if necessary but do not boil if using single (light) cream. Serve the sauce separately.

# Partridge with Parma ham and morels
### (Perdrix aux Morilles)
#### Serves 4

| METRIC/IMPERIAL | U.S. |
|---|---|
| 50 g/2 oz dried morels | 2 oz |
| milk and water for soaking | |
| 4 partridges | 4 |
| 50 g/2 oz butter/vegetable margarine | 4 tbsp |
| 8 slices of Parma ham | 8 |
| 1 wineglass red wine | 1 wineglass |
| 2 shallots | 2 |
| 1 stalk of celery | 1 |
| ½ wineglass brandy | ½ wineglass |
| fine sea salt and freshly ground black pepper | |
| 300 ml/½ pint double (heavy) cream, | |
| optional or single (light) | 1¼ cups |

Soak the morels in half milk, half water for about 12 hours. Drain and wash them well under running water; they usually grow in rather sandy soil and therefore need thorough cleaning. They are so delicous and the fragrance from them so splendid that they are worth the trouble.

Preheat the oven to 180°C/350°F/Mark 4.

Wipe the partridges well inside and out, then brown them gently in half of the butter or oil in a frying pan. Wrap each bird in a slice of Parma ham (anchor with a wooden toothpick, if necessary) and place them in a small flameproof casserole. Add the red wine, and the shallots and celery which you have sliced finely. Flame the brandy. Add this to the casserole and season to taste with salt and pepper. Cook for 1 hour to 1 hour 20 minutes.

Meanwhile, sauté the morels in the remaining butter. Add to the casserole for the last 20 minutes of cooking. For those who wish, the sauce can be enriched by adding the cream at the same time as the morels.

Taste the sauce and adjust the seasoning. Serve the partridges direct from the casserole.

# Partridge with lentils
### Serves 4

| METRIC/IMPERIAL | U.S. |
| --- | --- |
| 450 g/1 lb continental (green or French) lentils | 2 ⅓ cups |
| 50 g/2 oz butter/vegetable margarine | 4 tbsp |
| 3 rashers streaky (fatty) bacon | 4 slices |
| 2 carrots | 2 |
| 2 onions | 2 |
| 4 partridges | 4 |
| 1 wineglass red wine | 1 wineglass |
| 1 sprig of thyme | 1 |
| 1 bay leaf | 1 |
| fine sea salt and freshly ground black pepper | |
| a few small sausages | |

This recipe works equally well with pheasant.

Soak the lentils for 1−2 hours.
Preheat the oven to 190°C/375°F/Mark 5.
Melt the butter in a flameproof casserole large enough to hold the partridges. Add the bacon, carrots and onions all of which you have chopped, and the partridges and turn until browned on all sides. Add the red wine, cover tightly and transfer to the oven.
Cook for 1 hour.
At the same time, boil the drained lentils in enough water to cover them well, with the thyme, bay leaf, the other onion, chopped, and salt and pepper to taste. When tender, drain.
At the end of 1 hour, add the lentils to the partridges. Reduce the oven temperatute to 170°C/325°F/Mark 3 and cook for 1 more hour. About 20 minutes before the end, add a few small sausages to the casserole.
Serve the partridges with sauce, lentils and sausages.

# MALLARD

Mallard is the variety of wild duck which is most readily available in supermarkets and stores. There are many others, such as widgeon or teal, which are good to eat, but unless you have either an exceptional game shop or butcher nearby or a hunter in the family, they are not easily come by.

A mallard is sufficient for two people, sometimes three. Its meat, being very lean, is dry; to combat this when cooking it is a good idea to place in the cavity some low fat cream cheese such as Petit Suisse, an apple or an onion, and a bunch of parsley.

Cooking time is extremly variable and will alter with the age of the bird and the method of cooking. A bird which is labelled oven-ready is intended to be fit for roasting. If you like it rare and bloody 20-30 minutes will be sufficient for a fresh young bird, but an older bird in a casserole may take 1-1½ hours.

As mallard is usually shot in marshy coastal regions it can have a 'fishy' flavour unless you take steps to reduce or eliminate this. In our experience, lightly poaching the bird for 20 minutes or so in salted water will take away this flavour. Make sure to rinse and dry the duck well before beginning the recipe.

Mallards can be frozen satisfactorily, but are at their best when eaten within two or three days of shooting.

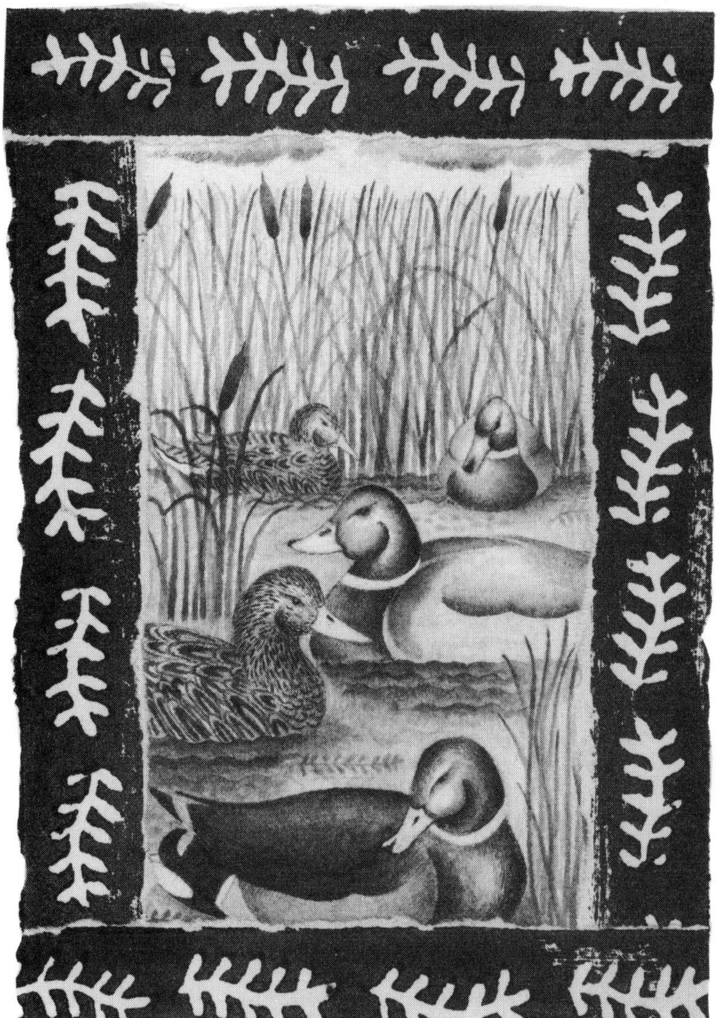

# Wild duck with turnips
(Canard sauvage aux navets)
Serves 4

| METRIC/IMPERIAL | U.S. |
|---|---|
| 2 young mallard | 2 |
| fine sea salt and freshly ground black pepper | |
| 75 ml/5 tbsp sunflower oil | 5 tbsp |
| 2 small apples | 2 |
| 300 ml/½ pint chicken stock | 1¼ cups |
| 2 wineglasses white wine | 2 wineglasses |
| 700 g/1½ lb turnips | 1½ lb |
| 12 medium shallots | 12 |
| 25 ml/1½ tbsp icing (confectioners') sugar | 1½ tbsp |
| 15 ml/1 tbsp white wine vinegar | 1 tbsp |
| redcurrant jelly, optional | |
| mustard and cress, to garnish | |

This is a recipe given by a dear friend from the Jura region of France. She has often cooked it for us, using Barbary duck — but we have varied it with mallard and found it worked well. Be sure you buy young birds and use very small round turnips. The flavour of large old turnips is too strong and will overwhelm the dish.

Preheat the oven to 230°C/450°F/Mark 8.
Season the cavities of the birds with salt and pepper and brown them in 30 ml/2 tbsp of oil. Put an apple inside each duck, and tuck in the tail ends. Place them in a roasting pan and pour in the stock and white wine. Roast for 20-30 minutes, basting frequently.
Meanwhile, blanch the turnips in a little boiling water. Drain and reserve. Blanch the shallots, drain and reserve. Heat the remaining oil in a small pan and add the sugar and turnips. Cook over a medium heat until the turnips start to brown and caramelise. This should take 10-15 minutes, depending on the size of the turnips. Add the shallots and continue cooking until both vegetables are browned and tender. Sprinkle with the vinegar — in a few minutes it will vapourise — then remove from the heat and keep warm.
When the ducks are cooked, remove from the roasting pan and place on a hot serving dish.

Surround with the vegetables and keep hot.
Reduce the stock in the roasting pan a little, taste and adjust
seasoning and, if desired, add some redcurrant jelly.
Sprinkle the ducks with mustard and cress and serve, with the
sauce separately.

# Roast wild duck
### Serves 4

| METRIC/IMPERIAL | U.S. |
|---|---|
| 2 young mallard | 2 |
| fine sea salt and freshly ground black pepper | |
| 2 small onions | 2 |
| bunch of parsley | |
| 25 g/1 oz butter/vegetable margarine | 2 tbsp |
| 1 wineglass red wine | 1 wineglass |
| 30 ml/2 tbsp sunflower oil | 2 tbsp |
| 6-8 rashers streaky (fatty) bacon | 8-10 slices |
| orange juice, optional | |
| flour for dredging | |

Preheat the oven to 230°C/450°F/Mark 8.
Season the cavities of the birds with salt and pepper, and place an
onion, ½ bunch of parsley and a nut of butter inside each bird.
Tuck in the tail ends. Pour the wine and oil into a roasting pan
and place the birds in it. Cover the breasts with the bacon.
Roast for about 20 minutes (rare) or 25-30 minutes (fairly well
done). Remember to baste the birds well several times. Some
orange juice may be added to the pan to help baste the birds.
About 5 minutes before they are ready, remove the bacon, baste
the breasts well and dredge with flour. Baste again, then return to
the oven and roast until the breasts of the birds are golden brown.

# Mallard in walnut and pomegranate sauce
### (Koreshe fesenjan)
### Serves 4

| METRIC/IMPERIAL | U.S. |
|---|---|
| 2 mallard | 2 |
| 45-60 ml/3-4 tsbp olive oil | 3-4tbsp |
| 1 large onion | 1 |
| 100 g/4 oz finely chopped walnuts | 1 cup |
| 150 ml/¼ pint fresh pomegranate juice | ⅔ cup |
| 450 ml/¾ pint chicken stock | 2 cups |
| 2.5 ml/½ tsp ground cinnamon | ½ tsp |
| 15 ml/1 tbsp brown sugar | 1 tbsp |
| fine sea salt and freshly ground black pepper | |
| lemon juice or sugar to taste | |
| 30 ml/2 tbsp tomato paste, optional | 2 tbsp |
| 225 g/8 oz coarsely chopped walnuts | 2 cups |
| pomegranate seeds, to garnish, optional | |

There are many versions of this delicious Iranian dish, and it can be made with wild duck, domestic duck or chicken. If you cannot buy fresh pomegranates to squeeze for the juice, you can use canned or bottled pomegranate juice or syrup, which is sold in Middle Eastern food shops. Do not use grenadine syrup: it is much too sweet. An alternative to pomegranage juice, that gives a sharper taste, is to use the juice of two lemons.

Cut the mallards into serving pieces and brown gently in 30 ml/2 tbsp of oil in a flameproof casserole or heavy saucepan. Remove and reserve. Add the remaining oil and the chopped onion and sauté until translucent. Add the finely chopped walnuts, pomegranate juice, chicken stock, tomato paste, cinnamon, sugar and salt and pepper to taste. Bring to the boil, stirring well. Return the ducks to the casserole making sure that the pieces are well covered by the sauce. Cover the pan and simmer for 50 minutes to 1¼ hours or until the ducks are very tender. Taste the sauce and adjust the seasoning: if too sweet, add lemon juice; if too tart, add a little sugar. Skim off excess fat. Place the ducks on a hot serving dish. Spoon over the sauce. Sprinkle on the coarsely chopped walnuts and any spare pomegranate seeds. Serve with Timman, page 115.

# Mallard with apples and ginger
Serves 4

| METRIC/IMPERIAL | U.S. |
|---|---|
| 2 young mallard | 2 |
| fine sea salt and freshly ground black pepper | |
| 2 small apples | 2 |
| 40 g/1½ oz softened butter/vegetable margarine | 3 tbsp |
| 30ml/2 tbsp sunflower oil | 2 tbsp |
| flour for dredging | |
| 4 firm dessert apples such as Cox's, Reinette, Winesap | 4 |
| 10 ml/2 tsp ground ginger | 2 tsp |
| 5 ml/1 tsp brown sugar | 1 tsp |
| 75 ml/3 fl oz Calvados | 6 tbsp |
| 150 ml/¼ pint single (light) cream | ⅔ cup |
| watercress, to garnish | |

Preheat the oven to 230°C/420°F/Mark 8.

Season the cavities with salt and pepper and put a small apple inside each of them. Rub the breasts with some of the softened butter. Tuck in the tail ends. Place in a roasting pan with a little of the oil and roast for 25-30 minutes; for those who like mallard rare 20 minutes will do. Baste often.

About 5 minutes before they are ready, baste the breasts well and dredge with flour. Baste again and return to the oven.

While the ducks are roasting, peel and quarter the dessert apples. Brown them in the remaining oil and butter, then sprinkle with the ginger and brown sugar. Keep warm.

Remove the ducks from the oven and keep warm. Pour off any fat from the roasting pan (leaving the sediment) and deglaze the pan juices with the Calvados. Strain into a small saucepan. Bring to the boil quickly and reduce a little. Add the cream and heat, taking care not to let the sauce boil. Taste for seasoning.

Carve the birds and arrange on a very hot serving dish with the quartered apples. Watercress, divided into sprigs, gives colour to the dish. Either pour the sauce on the ducks or serve it separately.

# Mallard with pimiento olives
## Serves 4

| METRIC/IMPERIAL | U.S. |
|---|---|
| 2 mallard | 2 |
| fine sea salt and freshly ground black pepper | |
| sunflower oil for frying | |
| 2 medium onions | 2 |
| 1 large onion | 1 |
| 2 large carrots | 2 |
| 1 bouquet garni comprising 3 parsley sprigs, 2 thyme sprigs and 1 bay leaf | 1 |
| 5 ml/1 tsp paprika, or more to taste | 1 tsp |
| 2 wineglasses port wine or Madeira | 2 wineglasses |
| 24 pimiento-stuffed olives | 24 |

Season the cavities of the ducks with salt and pepper. Heat the oil in a frying pan and brown the ducks all over. Remove from the pan. Cut the medium onions in half and put two halves into the cavity of each duck. Tuck in the tail ends.

Thickly slice the large onion and the carrots and brown quickly in the oil in the frying pan. Drain and spread in the bottom of a heavy casserole. Add the bouquet garni. Place the ducks on top of this vegetable bed. Mix the paprika with the port or Madeira and pour over the ducks. Cover the casserole with foil and the lid and cook gently for 60-90 minutes on top of the stove or in a preheated 180°C/350°F/Mark 4 oven. Baste frequently.

Meanwhile, blanch the olives in boiling water for 3 minutes, drain and soak in cold water for 20 minutes.

Remove the ducks to a hot serving dish and keep hot. Strain the vegetables and cooking liquid through a sieve, pressing the mixture through the sieve with the back of a spoon. Throw away the residue. Skim any fat from the surface of the sauce. Drain the olives and add them to the sauce. Reheat, and taste and adjust the seasoning.

Serve the ducks with the sauce.

# Mallard in Grand Marnier sauce
## Serves 4

| METRIC/IMPERIAL | U.S. |
|---|---|
| 2 mallard | 2 |
| flour for coating | |
| fine sea salt and freshly ground black pepper | |
| sunflower oil for frying | |
| 1 small orange | 1 |
| 6 large oranges | 6 |
| 125 ml/4 fl oz Grand Marnier | ½ cup |
| 10 ml/2 tsp brown sugar | 2 tsp |

This is a simple recipe for an older bird which needs to be casseroled.

Preheat the oven to 180°C/350°F/Mark4.
Season the cavities with salt and pepper and roll the birds in flour. Brown them all over in heated oil. Cut the small orange in half and put a half in each bird. Tuck in the tail ends, and arrange in a medium casserole. Pour over the juice of four of the oranges and season well with salt and pepper. Cook in the oven for 1½-2 hours, basting frequently with the juice.
Meanwhile, pare the rind from the two remaining oranges and cut it into julienne strips. Blanch in boiling water and drain well. Peel all the white pith from the two oranges and divide them into skinned segments; reserve. Place the julienne strips of orange rind, Grand Marnier and sugar in a saucepan and bring to the boil quickly. Simmer for a few seconds.
When the birds are cooked, remove them from the casserole and keep hot. Add the juices from the casserole to the Grand Marnier sauce, bring back to a simmer and taste for seasoning. Warm the orange segments in a non-stick pan.
Discard the halves of orange from the duck cavities. Cut the ducks in halves, place them on a hot serving plate and garnish with the warmed orange segments. Serve the sauce separately.

# GROUSE

Of the many species of grouse, the red grouse, from Scotland and the North of England, is the one of which such a fuss is made on 'The Glorious Twelfth', (the 12th August is the date set for the beginning of the season for shooting feathered game). The race to present these birds on the restaurant tables of London and Paris arouses almost as much ballyhoo as the race in the opposite direction to sell Beaujolais Nouveau to the North.

Among the other varieties, black grouse can be twice as large and ptarmigan, which turns white in winter, much smaller. In North America there are many species such as ruffed grouse, blue grouse and prairie chicken. In general, allowing different cooking times for the variations in size, similar recipes and similar accompaniments to those used for red grouse or pheasant can be used.

Grouse have dark meat but a much stronger flavour than many of the other game birds. They are at their best from in early autumn by which time they will probably be large enough to chop in two. If frozen at the right time they freeze quite well.

# Roast grouse
Serves 4

| METRIC/IMPERIAL | U.S. |
|---|---|
| 4 grouse | 4 |
| 50 g/2 oz butter/ vegetable margarine | 4 tbsp |
| 4 rashers streaky (fatty) bacon | 4 slices |
| 4 slices of toasted bread | 4 |
| 30 ml/2 tbsp sunflower oil | 2 tbsp |
| flour for dredging | |
| 60 ml/4 tbsp port or red wine | ¼ cup |
| fine sea salt and freshly ground black pepper | |
| watercress, to garnish | |

Preheat the oven to 220°C/425°F/Mark 7.
Wipe the birds inside and out and put a quarter of the butter in
each cavity. Truss and tie a slice of bacon on each bird. Cut the
corners off the toast to make each piece the size of a bird and place
in a roasting pan. Stand the birds on the toast and pour the oil
over. Roast for 25-35 minutes. Baste frequently.
About 10 minutes before the birds are ready, remove the bacon,
dredge the breasts with flour and baste. When the birds are
cooked, remove each one on its croûte to a hot serving dish.
To make the sauce, pour away most of the fat from the roasting
pan and add the port or red wine to deglaze. Bring to the boil,
scraping up the sediment. Adjust the seasoning.
Garnish the grouse with watercress and serve with the sauce.

# Grouse pot-roasted in red wine
(Grouse en cocotte)

Serves 4

| METRIC/IMPERIAL | U.S. |
|---|---|
| 2 grouse | 2 |
| 40 g/1½ oz butter/ vegetable margarine | 3 tbsp |
| 3 onions | 3 |
| 3 carrots | 3 |
| 2 stalks of celery | 2 |
| 2 small white turnips | 2 |
| 1 bouquet garni comprising 1 sprig of parsley, 1 sprig of thyme and 1 bay leaf | 1 |

| | |
|---|---|
| *2 wineglasses red wine* | *2 wineglasses* |
| *150 ml/¼ pint stock* | *⅔ cup* |
| *fine sea salt and freshly ground black pepper* | |

Preheat the oven to 170°C/325°F/Mark 3.
Wipe clean and dry the grouse. Melt the butter in a flameproof casserole and brown the birds. Remove and reserve. Slice the onions, carrots and celery, and cut the turnips into cubes. Add the vegetables to the casserole and sauté.
Place the grouse on top of the vegetables. Add the bouquet garni, wine, stock, and salt and pepper to taste. Bring to the boil, then cover and cook in the oven for 1½-2 hours or until tender.
Adjust the seasoning and serve, with croûtons of wholemeal (whole wheat) bread and cranberry jelly.

## Grouse with mushrooms
Serves 4

| METRIC/IMPERIAL | U.S. |
|---|---|
| *2 grouse* | *2* |
| *40 g/1½ oz butter/vegetable margarine* | *3 tbsp* |
| *2 onions* | *2* |
| *4 rashers lean bacon* | *4-6 slices* |
| *4 juniper berries* | *4* |
| *150 ml/¼ pint stock* | *⅔ cup* |
| *1½ wineglasses medium sherry or* | |
| *Madeira* | *1½ wineglasses* |
| *fine sea salt and freshly ground black pepper* | |
| *12 medium mushrooms* | *12* |

Preheat the oven to 180°C/350°F/Mark 4.
Wipe the grouse inside and out. Heat the butter in a flameproof casserole and brown the grouse well. Remove and keep warm.
Add the sliced onions to the casserole and sauté until golden brown. Place the grouse on the onions and cover the birds with the bacon. Add the crushed juniper berries, stock, sherry and salt and pepper to taste. Bring to the boil, then cover and cook in the oven for 1½-2 hours or until tender.
About 20 minutes before the grouse are ready, add the mushrooms.
When ready, split each grouse in half and serve on a very hot dish. Taste the sauce for seasoning, and spoon over the birds.

# VENISON

Deer farming was among the earliest of all animal husbandry, and deer farms and parks were familiar until the seventeenth century. After that, new farming methods concentrated on richer, fattier yields from beef and mutton.

Today, we are moving away from high fat meats for many reasons, chiefly health concerns and the desire to stay slim. Venison farming has arisen again to supply a meat that can make a modern diet healthier, yet full of variety and flavour.

Red deer, fallow deer and roe deer are the three kinds of vension most frequently on the market. The red deer, the largest, has the strongest flavour for those who like it, while the roe deer, is the most tender and delicate in texture, the *chevreuil* of good French restaurants. In North America, the meat of other antlered species — moose, elk, caribou and antelope — is also sold as venison.

The best joints are the haunch and saddle — the leg and loin. These are usually roasted or braised, or used to supply medallions (fillet steaks). Hunted venison is often of doubtful age, and for this reason the meat is usually marinated in oil or wine and spices before cooking, to tenderise and reduce some of the strong gamey flavour. Farmed venison is sold at about one and a half years old, and the meat should be more predictably tender. However, when in any doubt, use a marinade. Farmed venison, having only a fraction of the fat content of beef or lamb, needs care in cooking and should never be over-done. Basting or larding also helps the meat to stay moist and tender.

The neck, the breast and the shoulder are the cuts best used for casseroles and stews, and produce rich, flavourful mixtures. Chops and steaks can be grilled (broiled) or fried, but they should always be under-done to preserve tenderness, and then 'rested' in a warm oven if there is any objection to the pink juices.

We allow 175-225 g/6-8 oz of boned venison and 275-350 g/10-12 oz of venison on the bone per person.

# Roast venison with apple and prune compote
Serves 4

| METRIC/IMPERIAL | U.S. |
|---|---|
| 1.4 kg/2 ½ lb boned and rolled haunch of venison, thinly barded with pork fat | 2 ½ lb |
| 30 ml/2 tbsp olive oil | 2 tbsp |
| 50 g/2 oz smoked lean bacon | 2 oz |
| 125 ml/4 fl oz port wine or Madeira | ½ cup |
| 15-30 ml/1-2 tbsp redcurrant jelly | 1-2 tbsp |
| fine sea salt and freshly ground black pepper | |
| MARINADE | |
| 1 medium carrot | 1 |
| 1 medium onion | 1 |
| 3 juniper berries | 3 |
| ½ bottle red wine | ½ bottle |
| 30 ml/2 tbsp olive oil | 2 tbsp |
| 15 ml/1 tbsp wine vinegar | 1 tbsp |
| 6 black peppercorns | 6 |
| 2 sprigs of parsley | 2 |
| APPLE AND PRUNE COMPOTE | |
| 3 cooking (tart) apples | 3 |
| 1 cm/½ inch piece of fresh root ginger | ½ inch |
| 8-12 pitted prunes | 8-12 |
| 300 ml/½ pint water | 1 ¼ cups |
| 15-30 ml/1-2 tbsp brown sugar | 1-2 tbsp |

For the marinade, peel and slice the carrot and onion and place them in a flat glass or pottery dish (never metal) with the crushed juniper berries. Add the other marinade ingredients and the venison. Cover and marinate in a cool place for 48 hours, turning the meat frequently in the marinade.

Preheat the oven to 180°C/350°F/Mark 4.

Remove the venison from the marinade and pat dry. Heat the oil in a flameproof casserole, add the venison and brown on all sides. Add the bacon cut into fairly large dice and brown. Strain the marinade and pour the liquid over the venison and bacon. Bring to simmering on top of the stove, then cover with a double layer of foil and put the lid on tightly.

Cook in the oven for 35 minutes per 450 g/1 lb.

Meanwhile, make the compote. Peel the apples and slice them. Peel the ginger and slice into small pieces. Put the apples and ginger together with the prunes, water and brown sugar into a small saucepan and simmer gently until the apples and prunes are soft. (This can be made 2-3 days ahead, and is also delicious served with other game.)

When done, remove the venison and keep warm. Strain the cooking liquid into a saucepan and boil to reduce by one-third. Add the port or Madeira and redcurrant jelly. Reduce again. Taste for seasoning. Serve the venison with the sauce and compote.

# Venison shepherd's pie
### Serves 4-6

| METRIC/IMPERIAL | U.S. |
|---|---|
| 450-700 g/1-1½ lb cold meat from cooked haunch of | |
| venison | 1-1½ lb |
| 2 medium onions | 2 |
| 15 ml/1 tbsp sunflower oil | 1 tbsp |
| 10 ml/2 tsp tomato paste | 2 tsp |
| 300 ml/½ pint good brown stock | 1¼ cups |
| 5 ml/1 tsp dried mixed herbs (oregano, parsley, | |
| bay leaf) | 1 |
| fine sea salt and freshly ground black pepper | |
| 450 g/1 lb puréed potato | 2 cups |
| 450 g/1 lb puréed parsnip | 2 cups |
| 25 g/1 oz butter | 2 tbsp |
| milk | |
| 1 size 2-3 (extra large) egg | 1 |

A good recipe should you ever have any cold left-over venison.

Preheat the oven to 180°C/350°F/Mark 4.

Finely dice or mince (grind) the venison, removing all gristle and skin. Chop the onions and fry in the oil until softened.

Mix the venison, onions, tomato paste, stock and herbs together. Add salt and pepper to taste. Put the mixture into a pie or baking dish. Cover with the puréed potatoes and parsnips, which you have mixed together with the butter, a little milk and the well beaten egg. Glaze the top with milk, then bake for about 45 minutes or until the pie is heated through and the top well browned.

# Venison goulash
Serves 4-6

| METRIC/IMPERIAL | U.S. |
|---|---|
| 900 g/2 lb boneless stewing venison | 2 lb |
| 2 large sweet red peppers | 2 |
| 1 medium onion | 1 |
| 2-3 cloves of garlic | 2-3 |
| 1 stalk of celery | 1 |
| flour for coating | |
| 45 ml/3 tbsp olive oil | 3 tbsp |
| 400 g/14 oz canned tomatoes | 14 oz |
| 30 ml/2 tbsp tomato paste | 2 tbsp |
| 30 ml/2 tbsp paprika | 2 tbsp |
| 5 ml/1 tsp caraway seeds | 1 tsp |
| fine sea salt and freshly ground black pepper | |
| 450 g/1 lb potatoes, optional | 1 lb |
| 300 ml/½ pint plain yoghurt | 1¼ cups |
| MARINADE | |
| 300 ml/½ pint red wine | 1¼ cups |
| 30 ml/2 tbsp olive oil | 2 tbsp |
| 1 onion | 1 |
| 1 medium carrot | 1 |
| 6 black peppercorns | 6 |
| 1 bay leaf | 1 |

In a shallow dish (china or glass but not metal), combine all the marinade ingredients, having first roughly chopped the onion and the carrot. Stir well and add the cubed venison. Cover and leave in a cool place for 12-24 hours, stirring and turning the venison cubes from time to time.

Cut the peppers in half and remove pith and seeds. Roughly chop the peppers into cubes. Roughly chop the onion and the garlic. Cut the celery into 1 cm/½ inch slices.

Remove the venison cubes from the marinade. Pat dry and roll in a little flour. Strain the marinade and reserve.

Heat the oil in a large frying pan, and brown the venison quickly. Remove it, then add the chopped vegetables to the oil and sauté quickly; but do not allow to brown.

Put the venison and fried vegetables into a flameproof casserole. Add the tomatoes, roughly chopped, and the tomato paste.

Sprinkle the paprika, caraway seeds, and salt and pepper to taste on to the contents of the casserole, and pour in the marinade liquid. Stir well and bring almost to boiling. Cover with a double piece of foil and press the lid down firmly. Turn down the heat and simmer gently on top of the stove for 1½-2 hours.

If you wish, 25 minutes before the goulash is ready, add the potatoes, peeled and cubed.

Just before serving, add the yoghurt and stir. Taste for seasoning: more paprika or caraway may be added if liked.

# Deer Manston
## Serves 4

| METRIC/IMPERIAL | U.S. |
|---|---|
| 900 g/2 lb boneless braising venison | 2 lb |
| 30 ml/2 tbsp olive oil | 2 tbsp |
| 26-30 cloves of garlic | 26-30 |
| 300 ml/½ pint cooking brandy | 1¼ cups |
| 150 ml/¼ pint water | ⅔ cup |
| fine sea salt and freshly ground black pepper | |
| 225 g/8 oz button mushrooms | ½ lb |

This dish was introduced to us by Sally Harrison, a wonderful cook, hostess and friend at Manston House in Dorset. It is delicious, and easily prepared for a large dinner party.

Slice the venison into long strips about 2 cm/¾ inch wide. Brown them in the heated oil in a frying pan, then remove from the pan and place in a flameproof casserole or saucepan. Add the peeled cloves of garlic, the brandy, water, and salt and pepper to taste. Bring to the boil, stirring slowly to amalgamate. Seal the pan with a double piece of foil and press the lid down firmly to fit tightly. Some condensation will form on the foil and drop on to the stove; this is nothing to worry about. Simmer on the lowest heat possible on the top of the stove for 2-2½ hours.

About 30 minutes before the venison has finished cooking, stir in the mushrooms.

# Venison in red wine sauce
### Serves 4

| METRIC/IMPERIAL | U.S. |
|---|---|
| 900 g/2 lb boneless braising venison | 2 lb |
| 3 carrots | 3 |
| 1 large onion | 1 |
| 60-75 ml/4-5 tbsp olive oil | 4-5 tbsp |
| 16 juniper berries | 16 |
| flour for coating | |
| fine sea salt and freshly ground black pepper | |
| 300 ml/½ pint red wine | 1¼ cups |
| 150 ml/¼ pint water | ⅔ cup |
| MARINADE | |
| 1 carrot | 1 |
| 1 small onion | 1 |
| 300 ml/½ pint red wine | 1¼ cups |
| 15 ml/1 tbsp wine vinegar | 1 tbsp |
| 3 sprigs of parsley | 3 |
| 6 black peppercorns | 6 |
| fine sea salt | |

A warm winter dish, this is easily served in quantity for a party.

For the marinade, cut the carrot and onion into slices and put into a flat shallow dish with the rest of the marinade ingredients. Cube the venison add to the marinade and cover. Leave in a cool place for 12-18 hours. Turn the meat over from time to time. Remove the venison from the marinade and pat dry. Strain the marinade and reserve only the liquid. Grate the carrots and slice the onion finely. Sauté the vegetables in the oil in a frying pan until light brown. Crush the juniper berries, stir into the vegetables and cook for a few minutes more. Remove the vegetable mixture from the oil with a slotted spoon and reserve. Roll the venison in flour seasoned with salt and pepper. Brown in the hot oil. Put the vegetable mixture and the venison into a flameproof casserole or saucepan.

Pour the marinade liquid into the frying pan and bring to the boil, scraping up the sediment as you stir. Add to the casserole together with the red wine, water, and salt and pepper to taste. Bring to the boil, then turn down the heat. Cover with a double layer of foil

and press the lid down firmly to fit tightly. Simmer on top of
stove on the lowest possible heat for 2-2½ hours.
Before serving, taste for seasoning.

# Venison casserole
(Geschmorte Hirschkeule)

Serves 4

| METRIC/IMPERIAL | U.S. |
|---|---|
| 6 rashers streaky (fatty) bacon | 8 slices |
| 1.2 kg/2½ lb joint of leg of venison for roasting | 2½ lb |
| fine sea salt and freshly ground black pepper | |
| 12 shallots | 12 |
| 225 g/8 oz mushrooms | ½ lb |
| 1 bay leaf | 1 |
| 8 juniper berries | 8 |
| 250 ml/8 fl oz red wine | 1 cup |
| 60 ml/4 tbsp cornflour (cornstarch) | ¼ cup |
| 125 ml/4 fl oz single (light)cream | ½ cup |

This German recipe is cooked in a *Romertöpf*, a casserole rather like
a chicken brick which must be soaked before use in the oven, but
then steams and bakes the meat with very tender results. Leg of
hare can also be cooked this way, adjusting the quantities
accordingly.

Soak the *Romertöpf* in cold water for at least 15 minutes.
Preheat the oven to 220°C/425°F/Mark 7.
Line the *Romertöpf* with the bacon. Season the venison with salt
and pepper and place on top. Add the chopped shallots, sliced
mushrooms, bay leaf, juniper berries and red wine. Cover and
cook in the oven for about 2½ hours.
Take out the meat and keep warm. Pour the cooking liquid into a
saucepan and thicken with the cornflour (cornstarch). Add the
cream with salt and pepper to taste and heat gently without
boiling. Serve the venison with the sauce.

# Venison Tourte
### (Tourte de chevreuil)
Serves 6-8

| METRIC/IMPERIAL | U.S. |
|---|---|
| 1.5-2 kg/3¼-4½ lb boneless haunch of venison, preferably roe deer | 3¼-4½ lb |
| 150 g/5 oz fat bacon or pork fat | 5 oz |
| fine sea salt and freshly ground black pepper | |
| 100 g/4 oz chicken livers | ¼ lb |
| butter for frying | |
| a little brandy, preferably fine champagne | |
| ½ bottle red wine | ½ bottle |
| short pastry, made with 300 g/12 oz (1½ cups) flour and 150 g/6 oz (¾ cup) butter, page 117 | |
| beaten egg to seal | |
| egg yolk to glaze | |
| STUFFING | |
| 80 g/3 oz pork fillet (tenderloin) | 3 oz |
| 80 g/3 oz veal fillet (tenderloin) | 3 oz |
| 50 g/2 oz chicken livers | 2 oz |
| butter for frying | |
| a little sherry | |
| fine sea salt and freshly ground black pepper | |
| 50 g/2 oz foie gras, marinated in a little brandy | 2 oz |
| 15 ml/1 tbsp Madeira | 1 tbsp |
| 15 ml/1 tbsp brandy | 1 tbsp |
| 100 ml/3½ fl oz single (light) cream | 7 tbsp |
| pinch of quatre-épices | |
| SAUCE | |
| venison or veal bones | |
| oil for frying | |
| 10 shallots | 10 |
| ½ bottle red wine | ½ bottle |
| 250 ml/8 fl oz veal stock | 1 cup |
| beurre manié to thicken | |
| fine sea salt and freshly ground black pepper | |

An exquisite dish, here given in a simplified version by Julien, the
chef of 'La Chaumière', a delightful small restaurant in Lauris-sur-
Durance, in Provence. Even this version is complex but well worth

the effort for a special occasion. And it's also well worth forgetting a low-fat diet for one evening.

Cut the venison into small cubes or strips. Cut the bacon or pork fat into similar pieces. Season with salt and pepper. Cut the chicken livers into quarters, and lightly fry in butter. Add the brandy and pour the chicken livers, butter and brandy over the venison and bacon. Lightly cover with a little red wine and leave to marinate for at least half a day.

To make the stuffing, finely chop or process the pork and veal. Chop the chicken livers, fry lightly in butter, and season with a little sherry and salt and pepper to taste. Add to the pork and veal with the foie gras, Madeira, brandy, cream, spice, and salt and pepper to taste. Mix to create a very light-textured stuffing. Check the seasoning carefully. (Fry a very small quantity in butter to taste the seasoning.) Set aside.

For the sauce, in a heavy frying pan, fry the bones in a little oil over a very fierce heat, then turn the heat down and add the coarsely chopped shallots and the red wine. Reduce it substantially. There should be very little liquid left. Add the veal stock and simmer for another 20 minutes, then strain the resulting sauce through a sieve. Add a little beurre manié to thicken, then season with salt and pepper to taste. When ready to serve, reheat the sauce, but do not boil.

Preheat the oven to 240°C/450°F/Mark 9.

Roll out the pastry to a thickness of 2.5 mm/⅛ inch and from this cut two discs, each about 25 cm/10 inches in diameter. Use one disc to line a glass, china or metal tart or quiche dish. (Julien makes the pie flat on a baking sheet, but we nervously prefer to have a dish to hold the whole together.) Spread one-half of the stuffing over the bottom, leaving a band of at least 1 cm/½ inch uncovered at the edge. Drain the venison, bacon or pork fat and chicken livers and place them on top, then cover with the remaining stuffing. Cover with the second disc of pastry and stick the edges together with beaten egg to seal them tightly. Brush the top of the pie with egg yolk, and garnish with some small leaves cut from the pastry remnants. Bake for 20 minutes, then reduce the oven temperature to 200°C/400°F/Mark 6 and bake for a further 25 minutes.

Bring to the table, cut and serve, serving the sauce separately. The perfume which arises from this classical dish is memorable.

# Marinated medallions of venison
## (Hirschmedaillons)
### Serves 4-6

| METRIC/IMPERIAL | U.S. |
|---|---|
| 10 juniper berries | 10 |
| 30 ml/2 tbsp sunflower oil | 2 tbsp |
| 900 g/2 lb fillet of venison (red deer) | 2 lb |
| 1 onion | 1 |
| 1 carrot | 1 |
| 2 wineglasses red wine | 2 wineglasses |
| 1 clove | 1 |
| 1 bay leaf | 1 |
| 1 sprig of rosemary | 1 |
| 300 ml/½ pint water | 1¼ cups |
| fine sea salt and freshly ground black pepper | |
| flour for coating | |
| butter or olive oil for frying | |
| 60-90 ml/4-6 tbsp single (light) cream | 4-6 tbsp |
| Roquefort cheese, optional | |
| 15 ml/1 tbsp blackcurrant jam | 1 tbsp |

A German recipe contributed by Ulf and Nadine Stelzenmüller.

Fry the crushed juniper berries in a little oil until they change colour slightly. Cool. Marinate the venison fillet in this oil and juniper mixture overnight, in a cool place.

Cut the venison fillet across into steaks, or medallions, about 2 cm/¾ inch thick. Trim the edges then set the medallions aside. Fry the venison trimmings in a little oil until brown and crispy.

Add the finely chopped onion and carrot and fry gently until golden brown. Pour in a glass of red wine, add the clove and herbs and reduce. Add the remaining red wine and simmer again, then pour in enough water so that the liquid becomes clear. Reduce again and strain. Put this sauce to one side.

Season the medallions with pepper, toss in flour and then fry in butter or olive oil until well browned and pink inside. Salt them and put on one side to keep warm.

Pour some of the sauce into the frying pan and scrape to mix in the meat juices. Add the cream, and stir to incorporate it into the sauce; do not allow to boil. A little Roquefort cheese can also be stirred in at this stage. Finally, add the blackcurrant jam. Pour the sauce over and serve with Chestnut Croquettes, p. 114.

# Venison steaks and chops

Steaks and chops can be cut from the leg or loin. The fillet steaks from young deer are delicious and tender and, we find, do not really need to be marinated before cooking. We prefer to quick fry them, rather than grill (broil), as this is more controllable and keeps them very moist.

Have fillet steaks, or medallions cut about 2 cm/¾ inch thick. Heat a very heavy frying pan over a high heat until almost red hot, then quickly add a mixture of butter and oil, allowing 7.5 ml/½ tbsp each for every two steaks. If they are large steaks or chops add more butter and oil, but not too much. Put the steaks in the pan. They will sear fast. Using a palette knife, not a fork, turn them over to brown the other sides. Then turn the heat down to medium and cook for a further 3-4 minutes on each side. Always undercook venison — serve a little pink. Remove the steaks to a hot dish and keep very hot while you add one of the mixtures below to the pan to make a sauce for the steaks.

1) 3 crushed juniper berries, 1 wineglass of red wine, and salt and pepper to taste: boil, then simmer for a few minutes, working all the residue from the steaks into the sauce.
2) A handful of seeded grapes, cut in half, 15 ml/1 tbsp of brandy, 1 wineglass of red wine, and salt and pepper to taste: boil and simmer, working in the residue.
3) 15 ml/1 tbsp of Dijon mustard, ½ wineglass of red wine, and salt and pepper to taste: boil and simmer, working in the residue, then add a little single (light) cream.
4) 3-4 spring onions (scallions), cut finely and cooked for a few seconds in a little butter in the pan, add 1 wineglass of dry white wine added and simmer, then stir in a little single (light) cream with salt and pepper to taste.

Cook large steaks or chops in the same way, but add 2 wineglasses of red wine, and salt and pepper to taste after the steaks have been seared. Simmer for 15-20 minutes, according to the size and taste.

# WILD BOAR

From being a menace to our primitive ancestors, and a feast to centuries of hunters, wild boar meat has now become something of a rarity. Boar finds its way on to restaurant menus in Belgium, Germany, Italy and France, and into homes where continental sportsmen or keen cooks have sought out its meat, where it is still served as a special occasion dish. In Sicily and Sardinia it is a more everyday meat, frequently eaten in the winter months.

Boar has been extinct in Britain since the eighteenth century, 'The Boar's Head' carol and other Christmas songs notwithstanding. The flavour of boar has been forgotten and most English cooks have been advised on ways to marinate pork 'in the manner of boar'. Only now are one or two enterprising breeders, most notably the Cambridge-based 'Wild Boar Company', reviving the strain in farm conditions.

In North America, there is a smaller version of the European boar, which is called peccary. When young it is very succulent.

The flavour of wild boar is very much appreciated, leaner and tougher and much stronger in taste than pork. As with many tougher kinds of 'game', a number of culinary traditions offer different ways of dealing with the meat, but many of the recipes include sharp fruits in the sauces or in the accompaniments to offset the powerful flavour of the main ingredient.

The meat of hunted wild boar must be served well-cooked, but farmed wild boar may be served pink.

# Roast wild boar
(Wildschweinbraten)
Serves 6−8

| METRIC/IMPERIAL | U.S. |
|---|---|
| 3 kg/6½ lb roasting joint of wild boar on the bone | 6½ lb |
| 100 g/4 oz butter/vegetable margarine | 1 stick |
| 250 ml/8 fl oz red wine | 1 cup |
| 3 pomegranates | 3 |
| 5 ml/1 tsp arrowroot | 1 tsp |
| 60 ml/4 tbsp single (light) cream | ¼ cup |
| fine sea salt and freshly ground black pepper | |
| 150 g/5 oz chopped blanched almonds | 1 cup |
| MARINADE | |
| 6 juniper berries | 6 |
| 6 allspice berries | 6 |
| 10 black peppercorns | 10 |
| 2 cloves | 2 |
| small bunch of rosemary | |
| 1 onion | 1 |
| 1 carrot | 1 |
| fine sea salt | |
| 1 litre/1¾ pints dry red wine | 1 quart |
| 1 orange | 1 |

This German recipe, an individual variation on a classic theme, was kindly given to us by Elke Vollstedt. The lean, pungent meat is served for special occasions and lingers long in the memory of her friends.

The marinade must be discarded after use, as the flavour becomes too strong to be incorporated in the final dish.

To make the marinade, crush the spices and rosemary in a mortar and put them in a heavy frying pan to dry roast. Turn them so that they do not burn, but merely intensify in strength. When they are heated and toasted, add the coarsely chopped onion and carrot, salt to taste and a little of the red wine to mix. Heat this gently to allow all the flavours to amalgamate. Cool, then add the coarsely chopped flesh and rind of the orange.

Put the marinade in an earthenware or china dish and add the boar, its skin removed. Cover with the remaining red wine. Cover the dish tightly and leave in a cool place for about 3 days, turning the meat from time to time. This will tenderise the meat and reduce some of the strong flavour.

Take the meat out of the marinade, dry it and discard the marinade.

Preheat the oven to 180°C/350°F/Mark 4.

Melt three-quarters of the butter in a roasting pan over a moderate heat, and lightly sear the outside of the boar. Do not cook over too high a heat or the meat will toughen.

Pour the red wine over the joint. Add the juice of two of the pomegranates. Roast the meat, basting from time to time, for 2½ – 3 hours. The meat must be well done: hunted wild boar's meat should not be eaten rare. The basting is also important with this very lean meat.

Remove the boar to a carving board and set aside in a warm place to rest before carving.

Strain the pan juices into a small saucepan. Mix a little of the juices with the arrowroot, then add to the saucepan and stir while heating gently. When thickened add the cream. Heat gently but do not boil. Season to taste with salt and pepper. Keep warm.

Toss the almonds in the remaining butter in a frying pan until golden brown. Remove the seeds from the third pomegranate. Carve and arrange the boar meat on a hot dish. Pour the sauce over the meat slices and garnish with the pomegranate seeds and almonds.

# Grilled minutes of wild boar
# with onion confit and sweet potatoes
Serves 4

| METRIC/IMPERIAL | U.S. |
|---|---|
| 4 escalopes (thin slices) cut from the haunch of wild boar | 4 |
| fine sea salt and freshly ground black pepper | |
| butter or olive oil for frying | |
| ONION CONFIT | |
| 450 g/1 lb button (pearl) onions | 1 lb |
| 45 ml/3 tbsp white wine vinegar | 3 tbsp |
| 100 g/4 oz clear honey | ⅓ cup |
| 30 ml/2 tbsp demerara (coarse brown) sugar | 2 tbsp |
| SWEET POTATO MOULDS | |
| 900 g/2 lb orange-fleshed sweet potatoes (yams) | 2 lb |
| juice of 2 lemons | |
| grated fresh root ginger to taste | |
| 45 ml/3 tbsp cream | 3 tbsp |
| 1 egg yolk | 1 |

In recent years, 'Rules' restaurant in London's Covent Garden has begun to serve wild boar along with its traditional English roasts, game pies and steak and kidney puddings. This recipe is a favourite with the chef, Graham Beauchamp, and clients alike. Although the meat of hunted wild boar should be well cooked, that of farmed wild boar may be served pink.

First make the onion confit. Place the onions in a pan with the vinegar. Bring to the boil and reduce the vinegar by half. Add the honey and sugar and simmer until the onions are soft and the sauce thick, dark and sticky.

Meanwhile, make the sweet potato moulds. Peel the sweet potatoes and remove any brown specks. Slice them 5 mm/¼ inch thick. Put in a saucepan, cover with water and add the lemon juice. Simmer until the potatoes are soft enough to mash. Drain well and mash. Mix in the ginger, cream and egg yolk. Fill greased dariole moulds with the mixture and keep warm.

Flatten the boar escalopes with a meat mallet or heavy weight until they are 5 mm/¼ inch thick. Season with salt and pepper. Grill (broil) or pan fry in a little butter or olive oil until well browned on both sides but still pink in the centre. Do not overcook. Rest for a minute, then serve with the onion confit arranged on each plate in a semi-circle around the escalopes and the unmoulded sweet potato garnish to one side.

# Wild boar steaks in a sweet and sour sauce
(Bistecche di cinghiale)
Serves 4

| METRIC/IMPERIAL | U.S. |
|---|---|
| 50 g/2 oz pitted prunes | ½ cup |
| 50 g/2 oz sultanas (golden raisins) | ⅓ cup |
| 60 ml/4 tbsp olive oil | ¼ cup |
| 100 g/4 oz streaky (fatty) bacon | ¼ lb |
| 700 g/1½ lb wild boar rib steaks | 1½ lb |
| 15 ml/1 tbsp flour | 1 tbsp |
| 300 ml/½ pint wine vinegar | 1¼ cups |
| 3 bay leaves | 3 |
| 30 ml/2 tbsp sugar | 2 tbsp |
| freshly grated nutmeg | |
| fine sea salt | |

Many regions of Italy feature wild boar on restaurant menus, but this is a speciality of Sardinia. The sweet and sour sauce also combines very well with venison.

Chop the prunes and put them to plump up with the sultanas (golden raisins) in a little warm water. Heat the olive oil in a frying pan and add the diced bacon. Fry until browned, then add the boar steaks to the pan and brown briskly on both sides. Turn down the heat and cook gently for about 15 minutes.
Mix the flour with half the vinegar in a small saucepan, then add the remaining vinegar, the bay leaves and sugar. Simmer gently, stirring to make a smooth sauce. Add the drained sultanas (golden raisins) and prunes, and nutmeg to taste. Cook gently for about 10 minutes.
Season the boar steaks with salt, then pour over the sauce. Cook for a further 10 minutes or until the steaks are tender.

# KID

In southern Europe – France, Italy and Greece – and in Latin America Easter kid is as much a sign of spring as Easter lamb is in northern countries. With the whole world seemingly competing for goat's cheese (even in France, cheese makers cannot get enough goat's milk and now make many cheeses from half goat's, half cow's milk), goat herds are a growing phenomenon, and questions about what to do with the meat are constantly arising. In Scotland and other parts where goats are bred for mohair production, the particularly tender meat is being introduced to local restaurants and finding acceptance.

Kid is, in flavour, like a very delicate, very lean lamb, though containing less than half the fat of lamb. For those who find venison too powerful a taste, this is the ideal delicate low-fat game meat.

Kid still has to be searched out at most butchers in Britain, although it is wholesaled by David Andrade and Sons Ltd at Smithfield Market, and obtainable from Scottish Goat Products, Ltd, of Newtonmore. In the United States, look for kid in ethnic markets.

# Gigot of kid baked in hay
### Serves 4-6

| METRIC/IMPERIAL | U.S. |
|---|---|
| 1.6 kg/3½ lb gigot (leg) of kid | 3½ lb |
| hay to cover generously | |
| 15 ml/1 tbsp chopped tarragon leaves | 1 tbsp |
| bunch of parsley | |
| fine sea salt and freshly ground black pepper | |
| 100 g/4 oz butter/vegetable margarine | 1 stick |
| 4 cloves of garlic | 4 |
| SAUCE | |
| 1 stalk of celery | 1 |
| 1 onion | 1 |
| 2 carrots | 2 |
| 50 g/2 oz dripping or | ¼ cup |
| 60 ml/4 tbsp oil | ¼ cup |
| 1 clove of garlic | 1 |
| 50 g/2 oz flour | 6 tbsp |
| 450 ml/¾ pint stock | 2 cups |
| 1 wineglass white wine | 1 wineglass |
| 15 ml/1 tbsp honey | 1 tbsp |

This recipe was kindly given to us by Alasdair Robertson, who serves it in the restaurant of The Holly Tree Hotel, Argyll, Scotland. Hay can be bought at gardening and pet shops.

Preheat the oven to 180°C/350°F/Mark 4.
Remove the hip bone and the end of the leg bone from the gigot. Put the bones into a roasting pan. Coarsely chop the celery, onion and carrots and add to the bones with the dripping or oil and garlic. Set aside.
Tie the hip end of the gigot for easier carving and place it in another large roasting pan. Cover the kid with hay, the tarragon and chopped parsley and add some salt and pepper. On top place the butter, cut into pieces. Bruise the peeled garlic cloves and place in one corner of the roasting pan. Cover the whole with foil and seal down well. Bake for 1 hour.
At the same time, place the pan with the bones and vegetables in the same oven to cook for 1 hour.
At the end of this time remove the pan of bones. Remove the foil and hay from the gigot and leave to cook for a further 25 minutes.

This achieves a nicely pink medium rare texture. Meanwhile, add the flour to the bones and pan juices. Add the wine. Stir well, then add the stock, and honey. Bring to the boil and reduce by one-third. Strain the resulting sauce, and adjust the seasoning. Remove the gigot from the oven and leave to rest in a warm place for 5-6 minutes. Carve and serve with the thin sweet and savoury sauce.

# Kid with artichokes

(Capretto e carciofi)
Serves 4—6

| METRIC/IMPERIAL | U.S. |
|---|---|
| 1.4 kg/3 lb boneless kid cut from the saddle | 3 lb |
| 150 ml/¼ pint olive oil | ⅔ cup |
| 1 onion | 1 |
| 50 g/2 oz cooked ham or bacon | 2 oz |
| 20 ml/4 tsp flour | 4 tsp |
| 300 ml/½ pint dry white wine | 1¼ cups |
| fine sea salt and freshly ground black pepper | |
| 6 small purple globe artichokes | 6 |
| juice of ½ lemon | |
| freshly chopped parsley | |

Cut the meat into 2.5 cm/1 inch chunks. Heat the oil in a flameproof casserole, add the meat and brown, turning, over a gentle heat. Stir in finely chopped onion and diced ham. Sprinkle the meat with the flour and continue stirring over a gentle heat. Add the wine and stir until it has amalgamated with the juices and come to the boil. Reduce a little.
Season to taste with salt and pepper. Put the lid on the casserole and cook over a low heat for 45 minutes.
Meanwhile, remove the stem and the outer leaves from the artichokes and cut the artichokes into quarters. Remove any tough looking choke from the centre. If the artichokes are large, slice them finely.
Add the artichokes to the casserole and cook for another 20 minutes or until both the meat and artichokes are tender. Check for seaoning, and add the lemon juice and parsley at the last moment before serving.

# Stuffed leg of kid in pastry
(Cabri farci en croûte)
Serves 4

| METRIC/IMPERIAL | U.S. |
|---|---|
| 900 g-1.4 kg/2-3 lb leg of kid | 2-3 lb |
| sunflower or olive oil for frying | |
| 1 large onion | 1 |
| 50 g/2 oz pine nuts | ⅔ cup |
| 8 dried apricots | 8 |
| 50 g/2 oz sultanas (golden raisins) | ½ cup |
| 2.5 ml/½ tsp ground cinnamon | ½ tsp |
| 1.25 ml/¼ tsp ground ginger | ¼ tsp |
| 2 eggs | 2 |
| fine sea salt and freshly ground black pepper | |
| 50 g/2 oz cooked rice | ½ cup |
| 350g/12 oz puff pastry, thawed if frozen | ¾ lb |

Ask your supplier to bone the leg of kid or, if you are dexterous and enjoy the challenge, bone it yourself, with a sharp knife.

Preheat the oven to 220°C/425°F/Mark 7.

In a frying pan, heat a little oil and sauté the finely chopped onion until soft. Add the pine nuts and brown, then add the apricots, which you have cut into small dice, the sultanas (golden raisins), cinnamon, ginger, and salt and pepper to taste. Stir for a few minutes until amalgamated and brown. Stir in the rice and add a beaten egg. Taste and add extra spices if required.

Stuff as much as possible of the cooled mixture into the cavity in the leg of the kid. Close with a skewer or sew with cooking string.

Place in a roasting pan on a rack and rub a little oil over the surface. Roast for 8 minutes on each side. Remove and set aside to cool slightly − 10 minutes is long enough.

Turn the oven temperature up 230°C/450°F/Mark 8.

Remove the skewer or string from the kid. Place the leg on a shallow greased baking tray. Roll out the pastry and cover the kid with it. Gently tuck the pastry around but not under the kid. Decorate with pastry trimmings. Lightly beat the egg with a little water and brush all over the pastry to glaze it.

Place in the oven and bake for 12 minutes or until the pastry is risen and brown. Turn down the oven temperature to 200°C/400°F/Mark 6 and bake for 15 minutes longer. Then turn the oven off, and leave the kid to rest for about 10 minutes.

# Spring casserole of kid
## (Ragoût de cabri)
### Serves 4

| METRIC/IMPERIAL | U.S. |
|---|---|
| 900g – 1.4kg/2 – 3lb breast of kid | 2 – 3lb |
| sunflower or olive oil for frying | |
| 2 large onions | 2 |
| 30 ml/2 tbsp flour | 2 tbsp |
| pinch of sugar | |
| 2 cloves of garlic | 2 |
| 30 ml/2 tbsp tomato paste | 2 tbsp |
| 1 bouquet garni comprising parsley, thyme and bay leaf | 1 |
| fine sea salt and freshly ground black pepper | |
| 16 small new potatoes | 16 |
| 100 g/4 oz shelled fresh peas | ⅔ cup |
| 100 g/4 oz shelled broad (fava) beans | scant ⅔ cup |
| 100 g/4 oz fine green beans | ¼ lb |
| freshly chopped parsley, to garnish | |

This is based on the wonderful French dish, Navarin de Mouton, which cooks mutton or lamb with spring vegetables.

Preheat the oven to 180°C/350°F/Mark 4.

Trim off any excess fat from the kid. With a sharp knife cut it into slices or riblets down the bones. Heat a little oil in a flameproof casserole and brown the pieces of kid. Remove from the pan and keep hot. Add the chopped onion and brown, then remove. Stir the flour and sugar into the fat in the casserole and cook until the mixture has browned.

Replace the meat and onions. Add the chopped garlic, tomato paste, bouquet garni, salt and pepper to taste, and enough water to cover the meat. Bring to simmering, then cover the casserole and place in the oven. Cook for 1 hour.

Remove from the oven. Allow the sauce to cool a little, then skim any excess fat from the surface. (The dish can be left at this point, and finished the next day.)

Add the potatoes, return to the oven and cook for another 35 minutes. Add the peas, broad (fava) beans and (green) beans, which you have cut in half, and cook for 15 minutes longer or until the vegetables are tender.

Serve from the casserole, with plenty of parsley sprinkled on top.

# SOUPS, TERRINES AND PIES

Most of the more readily available game lends itself to the making of the most splendid soups, terrines and pies. Moreover, it can be combined with other meats as in Grouse, Steak and Pigeon Pie and Pigeon, Hare and Ham Terrine.

The flavour of terrines is enhanced if kept for a couple of days before eating, but once cut the sooner eaten the better. It is worth remembering to take a terrine or pâté out of the refrigerator well before it is to be served — a chilled pâté can be quite tasteless. A kilo/2.2 lbs terrine is usually sufficient for 12 people as a first course and 6 if it is the main course.

Contemporary shopping often makes it extremely difficult to accumulate sufficient bones and other ingredients to make a really good stock. As the fine flavour of many game dishes has its origins in the stock, it is worth the effort to overcome these difficulties. If this is not possible resort to the ubiquitous, but very handy, stock (bouillon) cube. But remember that cubes are salty, so adjust the seasoning accordingly. Stock, once made, should be cooled fast and kept in the refrigerator but brought out and thoroughly boiled each day. For longer storage, it can be frozen.

# Game stock

METRIC/IMPERIAL                                          U.S.
*raw bones and any trimmings from the animal or bird*
*oil for frying*
*2-3 slices of ham or bacon*                            *2-3*
*onions*
*celery*
*leeks*
*carrot*
*calf's foot or pig's trotters (feet) if possible*
*sprigs of parsley*
*bay leaf*
*cloves*
*black peppercorns*
*juniper berries*

Chop the bones and brown the pieces well in hot oil in a large, deep pan or stockpot. Chop the ham or bacon and all the vegetables and add to the pan. Sweat a little, then add the calf's foot or pigs trotters, the herbs and spices, and sufficient water to cover. Bring to the boil, skimming off the scum. Cover, turn down the heat and simmer gently for 2-3 hours. Strain and cool.

# Game soup

Make the stock but do not strain it. Remove all the bones and calf's foot or pig's trotters from the stock. Liquidise the remainder, then pass it through a sieve. Add a wineglass of port wine and simmer. Check the seasoning. Serve very hot with a sprinkle of freshly chopped mixed herbs.

# Game and vegetable soup

Season the strained game stock. Add any small scraps of cooked game you may have, plus diced carrots, turnips and shallots. Pour in a wine-glass of port wine, sherry or Madeira and simmer until the vegetables are tender. Serve very hot, garnished with small croûtons, which have been fried with tiny cubes of bacon and sliced mushrooms, and a sprinkle of chopped chives on top.

103

# Pigeon, hare and ham terrine

| METRIC/IMPERIAL | U.S. |
|---|---|
| *1 hare* | *1* |
| *the breasts of 2 pigeons* | |
| *150 ml/¼ pint dry white wine* | *⅔ cup* |
| *60 ml/4 tbsp Cognac* | *¼ cup* |
| *4 juniper berries* | *4* |
| *2 shallots* | *2* |
| *oil for frying* | |
| *100 g/4 oz pork fat* | *¼ lb* |
| *5 ml/1 tsp dried thyme* | *1 tsp* |
| *1 egg* | *1* |
| *fine sea salt and freshly ground black pepper* | |
| *350-450 g/¾-1 lb tissue-thin slices of pork fat or* | |
| *unsmoked streaky (fatty) bacon* | *¾-1 lb* |
| *225 g/8 oz good quality cooked ham, in 2.5cm/1 inch* | |
| *cubes* | *½ lb* |
| *aspic powder or powdered (unflavoured) gelatine, to* | |
| *thicken* | |
| *gherkins and bay leaf, to garnish* | |

Remove all the meat from the hare and place it together with the skinned, boned and lightly beaten pigeon breasts in a bowl. Add the wine, and Cognac and crushed juniper berries and leave to marinate in a cool place overnight or for 48 hours if possible.

Turn the meat frequently.

Drain the meat and pat dry.

Strain the marinade and reserve the liquid.

Preheat the oven to 190°C/375°F/Mark 5.

Slice the shallots and sauté them lightly in oil. Reserve 5-6 large pieces of hare, and the pigeon breasts and cut into strips. Mince (grind) the rest of the hare meat, the shallots and pork fat. Add the thyme, marinade, beaten egg and salt and pepper to taste, and mix well.

Line a terrine dish with the thin pork fat or bacon. Stretching the fat thin can be done easily by holding it down on a board, and running the back of a carving knife across it. Spread the minced (ground) mixture on the bottom of the terrine, then place strips of marinated hare, pigeon and ham on top. Continue adding layers of the minced (ground) mixture and hare, pigeon and cubes of ham. Make sure that the last layer is the minced (ground) mixture. Cover with a layer of fat and the lid. Cook in a bain marie (a roasting pan with 5cm/2 inches of water will work just as well) for 1¼-1½ hours.

When cooked, the terrine will have shrunk from the sides of the dish. Pierce the terrine with a skewer: if there is no trace of blood and the juices run clear the terrine is done.

Remove the lid, place a weight on top and cool, preferably overnight, before serving. Sometimes we pour off the juices, thicken them with a little aspic powder or gelatine and pour them back over the terrine before cooling. The flavour of the terrine improves if kept for 3-4 days before serving.

Before serving, remove the top layer of fat and decorate with gherkins and a bay leaf.

# Simple rabbit pâté
### (Pâté de lapin)

| METRIC/IMPERIAL | U.S. |
|---|---|
| 1 kg/2¼ lb boneless rabbit | 2¼ lb |
| 350 g/12 oz belly of pork (fresh pork side) or other fat pork cut | ¾ lb |
| 12 small shallots | 12 |
| 1 large head of garlic | 1 |
| 15 ml/1 tbsp sea salt | 1 tbsp |
| 10 ml/2 tsp freshly ground black pepper | 2 tsp |
| 1 liqueur glass cooking brandy | 1 liqueur glass |
| sprigs of thyme or bay leaves, to garnish | |

Preheat the oven to 200°C/400°F/Mark 6.

Process or mince (grind) all the ingredients except the brandy and herbs. Add the brandy and stir in. Pack into a terrine dish lined with fat and garnish the top with herbs. Cover with fat and a tightly fitting lid and place the terrine in a bain-marie (a roasting pan with 5 cm/2 inches of water will work just as well).

Cook for 30 minutes, then reduce the oven temperature to 170°C/325°F/Mark 1, and cook for a final 30 minutes.

Remove fat and decorate with bay leaves and fresh thyme. Store for 1-2 days before serving.

# Rabbit in parsley
(Lapin persillé)
Serves 4-6

| METRIC/IMPERIAL | U.S. |
| --- | --- |
| 1 rabbit | 1 |
| milk for soaking, if necessary | |
| 300 ml/½ pint dry white wine | 1¼ cups |
| 450 ml/¾ pint chicken stock | 2 cups |
| 4 shallots | 4 |
| 4 small carrots | 4 |
| 1 bay leaf | 1 |
| 6 black peppercorns | 6 |
| 4 rashers smoked bacon | 4 slices |
| large bunch of parsley | |
| 1-2 cloves of garlic | 1-2 |
| fine sea salt and freshly ground black pepper | |
| 7.5 ml/1½ tsp powdered (unflavoured) gelatine | 1½ tsp |
| 10 ml/2 tsp lemon juice | 2 tsp |
| 3-4 thin slices of lemon | 3-4 |

Cut the rabbit into joints and soak it for about 12 hours in salted water. Drain, rinse and pat dry. Put the rabbit, wine, chicken stock, two of the shallots and the carrots cut in half, the bay leaf and peppercorns into a saucepan, cover and simmer gently for about 45 minutes to 1 hour or until tender. Allow to cool. Strip the meat from the bones and cut it into 1 cm/½ inch pieces. Strain the stock; reserve the liquid and the carrots. Cut the bacon into fine strips about 2.5 cm/1 inch long and poach gently for a few minutes in some of the stock together with the remaining shallots, sliced thickly. Remove and reserve.

Chop the parsley, and garlic and mix together in a bowl. Add the rabbit with the bacon strips, sliced shallots, half of the carrots cut into thin rings, and salt and pepper to taste.

Boil the stock to reduce to about 600 ml/1 pint (2½ cups). Cool slightly then put a little stock into a cup. Sprinkle the gelatine over and stir very briskly until thoroughly dissolved. Add the gelatine mixture to the remaining stock and mix well, then stir in the lemon juice and salt and pepper to taste. The stock should have a good strong flavour.

Put the rabbit mixture in a 1.2 litre/2 pints (5 cups) capacity glass bowl or soufflé dish and pour the stock gently over. Garnish the top with the remaining carrot and lemon slices. Chill until set. This dish is best served from the bowl.

# Pheasant pie
Serves 4

| METRIC/IMPERIAL | U.S. |
|---|---|
| the breasts of 3 pheasants | |
| 225 g/8 oz good cooked ham | ½ lb |
| 75 ml/5 tbsp red wine | 5 tbsp |
| 75 ml/5 tbsp cooking brandy | 5 tbsp |
| large bunch of parsley | |
| 2 medium shallots | 2 |
| 2 sprigs of thyme or | 2 |
| 2.5 ml/½ tsp dried thyme or marjoram | ½ tsp |
| 15 ml/1 tbsp olive oil | 1 tbsp |
| 20 g/¾ oz butter | 1½ tbsp |
| 150 g/6 oz mushrooms | 6 oz |
| fine sea salt and freshly ground black pepper | |
| 1 bay leaf | 1 |
| 125 ml/4 fl oz chicken stock | 1 |
| short pastry, made with 225 g/8 oz /1¼ cups) flour, page 117 | |
| 1 egg yolk | 1 |

Place the skinned and boned pheasant breasts, the ham cut into small pieces, wine, brandy, finely chopped parsley, chopped shallots, and thyme into a bowl (not metal) and marinate in a cool place overnight. Drain the pheasant breasts and pat dry. Reserve the ham and marinade.

Preheat the oven to 200°C/400°F/Mark 6. Sauté the pheasant breasts in the olive oil and a nut of the butter until lightly browned. In a pie dish, make a layer of the ham, then place the pheasant breasts on top. Pour over this all of the marinade mixture. Add the quartered mushrooms and salt and pepper to taste. Add the bay leaf, chicken stock and remaining butter. Cover with the pastry and make vents in the lid to allow the steam to escape. Beat the egg yolk with a pinch of salt and brush the mixture over the pastry — this will help to give it a rich, dark brown colour.

Bake for 20 minutes. When the pastry begins to brown, reduce the oven temperature to 180°C/350°F/Mark 4 and bake for a further 45 minutes. If the pastry appears to be browning too much, cover with a piece of damp greaseproof or parchment paper.

# Pheasant and pistachio terrine

| METRIC/IMPERIAL | U.S. |
|---|---|
| 1 large pheasant | 1 |
| 125 ml/4 fl oz Cognac | ½ cup |
| 125 ml/4 fl oz medium sherry | ½ cup |
| 1 onion | 1 |
| 1 carrot | 1 |
| 2.5 ml/½ tsp dried oregano | ½ tsp |
| 3-4 sprigs of parsley | 3-4 |
| 100 g/4 oz boneless veal | ¼ lb |
| 100 g/4 oz boneless pork | ¼ lb |
| 1 clove of garlic | 1 |
| 1 egg | 1 |
| 15 ml/1 tbsp single (light) cream, optional | 1 tbsp |
| 2.5 ml/½ tsp freshly grated nutmeg | ½ tsp |
| fine sea salt and freshly ground black pepper | |
| 50 g/2 oz shelled pistachio nuts | ⅓ cup |
| 350-450 g/¾-1 lb tissue-thin slices of pork fat or unsmoked streaky (fatty) bacon | ¾-1 lb |

Remove all the meat from the pheasant. Make sure that the pieces from the breast are cut in long slices. Put the meat in a bowl and add the Cognac, sherry, chopped onion and carrot, the oregano and parsley. Mix well, cover and leave to marinate in a cool place, preferably overnight.

Drain the meat and pat dry. Strain the marinade and reserve the liquid.

Preheat the oven to 190°C/375°F/Mark 5.

Reserve the slices of pheasant breast meat. Mince (grind) the rest of the meat, together with the veal, pork and garlic. Add the marinade, beaten egg, cream, nutmeg, and salt and pepper to taste. Put through the mincer (grinder) again or use a blender or food processor. The mixture should be very smooth.

To peel the pistachios, cover them with boiling water and leave for about 1-2 minutes, then drain. Rub gently between towels or kitchen paper to remove the skins. Chop the nuts roughly.

Line a terrine dish with the pork fat or bacon. Spread some of the minced (ground) mixture on the bottom. Place strips of pheasant breast on top and sprinkle on some chopped pistachios. Continue adding layers of the mixture, the pheasant and pistachios, finishing with a layer of the minced (ground) mixture. Cover with a layer of pork fat and the lid. Cook in a bain marie (a roasting pan with 5 cm/2 inches of water will work just as well) for 1¼-1½ hours.

Remove the lid and replace with a weight which presses down on to the terrine. Cool. Leave for 1-2 days in the refrigerator before serving.

# Grouse, steak and pigeon pie
### Serves 4

| METRIC/IMPERIAL | U.S. |
|---|---|
| 2 medium grouse | 2 |
| 225 g/8 oz tender steak such as rump or boneless sirloin | ½ lb |
| the breasts of 2 pigeons | |
| 3 rashers lean bacon | 3 slices |
| 2 shallots | 2 |
| 100 g/4 oz mushrooms | ¼ lb |
| 2 hard-boiled eggs | 2 |
| fine sea salt and freshly ground black pepper | |
| 200-300 ml/⅓-½ pint stock | ⅞-1¼ cups |
| short pastry, made with 225 g/8 oz (1¼ cups) flour, page 117 | |
| beaten egg to glaze | |

A variation of this dish uses hare and lamb's kidneys.
Preheat the oven to 200°C/400°F/Mark 6.
Cut the grouse into joints. Slice the steak into strips. Beat the skinned and boned pigeon breasts and cut each in half.
In a deep pie dish or casserole, make a layer of grouse, then steak and then pigeon. Scatter over the diced bacon, sliced shallots, quartered mushrooms, sliced eggs, and salt and pepper to taste. Repeat the layering until the dish is full. Add enough stock to three-quarters fill the dish.
Cover with the pastry, and make vents in the lid to allow the steam to escape, glaze with beaten egg and bake for 20-25 minutes. Reduce the oven temperature to 180°C/350°F/Mark 4 and bake for a further 1¼ hours. Cover the dish with damp grease-proof or parchment paper or foil, if it is browning too quickly.
This pie can be served either hot or cold.

# ACCOMPANIMENTS

## Redcurrant jelly

| METRIC/IMPERIAL | U.S. |
| --- | --- |
| 450 g/1 lb redcurrants | 1 lb (2 pints) |
| 150 ml/¼ pint water | ⅔ cup |
| sugar | |

Take the fruit from the stalks, wash and put into a preserving
pan with the water. Simmer the fruit to a pulp.
Put the pulp into a muslin cloth, over a preserving pan or large
bowl and allow the liquid to drip into the pan for some hours.
Measure the juice produced and add
450 g/1 lb (2¼ cups) of sugar for every 600 ml/1 pint (2½ cups) of
redcurrant juice. Boil until set point is reached, then pour into
small pots and seal.

## Cumberland sauce

| METRIC/IMPERIAL | U.S. |
| --- | --- |
| thinly pared rind of 1 lemon | |
| thinly pared rind of 2 oranges | |
| 225-275 g/8-10 oz redcurrant jelly | ¾-1 cup |
| 15 ml/1 tbsp Dijon mustard | 1 tbsp |
| fine sea salt and freshly ground black pepper | |
| 150 ml/¼ pint port wine | ⅔ cup |
| ground ginger, cayenne pepper or Grand Marnier, | |
| optional | |

A very simple and quick version.
Pare the rind from the lemons and oranges as thinly as possible.
Slice it into very thin strips and blanch them in boiling water for
4-5 minutes; drain. In a non-stick saucepan or bain-marie,
combine the jelly, strips of rind and mustard. Add a little salt
and pepper and let the jelly melt gently. A low heat is best. Stir
in port and heat through.
A pinch of ginger or cayenne pepper or even a little Grand
Marnier can vary the flavour.

# Apples with cardamom and cinnamon
Serves 4

| METRIC/IMPERIAL | U.S. |
|---|---|
| 4 cooking (tart) apples | 4 |
| 50 g/2 oz butter/vegetable margarine | 4 tbsp |
| 100 g/4 oz dark brown sugar | ½ cup |
| seeds from 4 green cardamom pods | |
| ground cinnamon | |

Peel, core and slice the apples. Melt the butter in a pan and add the apples. Cook until soft but not disintegrating. Add the sugar and the cardamom seeds and sprinkle with cinnamon. Cook, stirring gently, until the sugar has melted.

# Rowan jelly

| METRIC/IMPERIAL | U.S. |
|---|---|
| rowan berries | |
| sugar | |
| pared rind of 1 lemon | |
| 2 cloves | 2 |

Take berries from stalks, wash and put into a preserving pan. Add enough water just to cover the berries. Simmer until pulpy. Put the pulp into a muslin cloth, and allow to drip over a large bowl. Measure the juice produced and add 450 g/1 lb (2¼ cups) of sugar to every 600 ml/1 pint (2½ cups) of juice. Add the lemon rind and cloves, and boil rapidly until set.

# Cranberry sauce

| METRIC/IMPERIAL | U.S. |
|---|---|
| 175 ml/6 fl oz water | ¾ cup |
| 100 g/4 oz sugar | ½ cup |
| 225 g/8 oz cranberries | 2½ cups |
| 15 ml/1 tbsp brandy | 1 tbsp |
| 30 ml/2 tbsp orange juice, optional | 2 tbsp |
| grated orange rind, optional | |

Put the water and sugar in a saucepan. Stir until the sugar has dissolved, then add the cranberries and bring to the boil. Cook for 5-10 minutes or until the berries begin to pop. Do not overcook them. Stir in the brandy. Leave to cool for 1 hour or so before serving.

# Pears in red wine and brandy
Serves 4

| METRIC/IMPERIAL | U.S. |
| --- | --- |
| 4 firm pears | 4 |
| 100 g/4 oz brown sugar | ½ cup |
| 90 ml/6 tbsp red wine | 6 tbsp |
| ml/tbsp water | tbsp |
| 4 cloves | 4 |
| 2.5 ml/½ tsp ground cinnamon | ½ tsp |
| 30 ml/2 tbsp brandy | 2 tbsp |

Normally served as a dessert, we like these pears as an accompaniment to game. We usually make them 2-3 days before needed because the flavour improves with keeping.

Peel the pears, but leave on the stalks. Put the pears, sugar, wine and a little water and spices into a heavy saucepan and bring to the boil. Turn the heat down, cover and simmer gently for 20-25 minutes. Using a slotted spoon, turn the pears frequently so they will colour evenly.
Add the brandy and continue to simmer until the pears are tender (a futher 30-40 minutes).
Lift the pears out of the pan with a slotted spoon and set aside. Reduce the liquid a little, then strain the liquid over the pears.

# Golden rösti
Serves 4

| METRIC/IMPERIAL | U.S. |
| --- | --- |
| 700 g/1½ lb potatoes | 1½ lb |
| 100 g/4 oz butter, plus a little oil | 1 stick |
| fine sea salt and freshly ground black pepper | |

This is one of the great dishes of Switzerland, and although there are many cantonal variations the simplest is the best.

Partly boil the potatoes. Drain and leave to cool.
About 45 minutes before you wish to serve, heat half of the butter or oil in a frying pan. (Add a little oil if to stop the butter from burning.) Roughly grate the potatoes and spread them over the bottom of the pan. Season to taste with salt and pepper. Cook for about 20 minutes. Take from the heat and put a plate face down on top of the potatoes.

Turn the pan over so that the potatoes rest like a cake on to plate. (The Swiss have special twin frying pans which hook together to make this inversion simpler.) Add the rest of the butter to the pan and slide the rösti back into it, uncooked side down. Add more salt and pepper and cook for a further 25 minutes or until the potato cake is golden brown and crisp on the outside and still slightly moist on the inside.
A variation is to add 125 g/4 oz of crisp diced bacon. Another is to add partly cooked chopped onions and bacon and 5 ml/1 tsp of cumin seeds.

# Aubergine Imman Bayeldi
Serves 6-8

| METRIC/IMPERIAL | U.S. |
|---|---|
| 6 medium aubergines (eggplants) | 6 |
| fine sea salt and freshly ground black pepper | |
| 350 g/12 oz onions | ¾ lb |
| 300 ml/½ pint olive oil | 1¼ cups |
| 400 g/14 oz canned tomatoes | 14 oz |
| 3 cloves of garlic | 3 |
| freshly chopped parsley | |
| sultanas (golden raisins), optional | |
| 2 tomatoes | 2 |
| 5 ml/1 tsp sugar, or more to taste | 1 tsp |

Cut the aubergines (eggplants) in half lengthways. Scoop out the pulp without damaging the shells, cut into cubes and reserve. Score the inside of the shells without cutting through them and sprinkle with salt. Cover with a plate and set aside.
Sauté the sliced onions in a little of the oil until softened. Add the pulp of the aubergines (eggplants), the tomatoes, crushed garlic, parsley, and salt and pepper to taste, with the rests of the oil, and cook gently for 5-10 minutes. At this point add the sultanas (golden raisins), if liked.
Preheat the oven to 170°C/325°F/Mark 3.
Oil a flat baking dish. Rinse and dry the aubergines (eggplants) shells and lay them in the dish. Fill each shell with the vegetable mixture, and if there is a surplus place it around the sides. Slice the tomatoes, and put a slice on each stuffed shell. Sprinkle with sugar. Bake for 1½-2 hours. Serve cold or lukewarm.

# Chestnut croquettes
### Serves 4-6

| METRIC/IMPERIAL | U.S. |
|---|---|
| 225 g/8 oz mashed potato | 1 cup |
| 450 g/1 lb canned unsweetened chestnut purée | 1 lb |
| 15 ml/1 tbsp Cognac | 1 tbsp |
| freshly grated nutmeg | |
| fine sea salt | |
| 1 egg | 1 |
| breadcrumbs for coating | |
| butter or oil for frying | |

A traditional German recipe.

Process or beat together the mashed potato and chestnut purée. Add the Cognac, and season with nutmeg and a little salt. Bind with the beaten egg.

Roll the mixture into small walnut-sized balls and coat in breadcrumbs. Fry in butter or oil until golden brown all over and piping hot. Drain on kitchen paper.

# Onions in spiced syrup
### Serves 4-6

| METRIC/IMPERIAL | U.S. |
|---|---|
| 600 g/1¼ lb button (pearl) onions | 1¼ lb |
| sea salt | |
| 45 ml/3 tbsp olive oil | 3 tbsp |
| 2 cloves | 2 |
| 3 white peppercorns | 3 |
| 1 bay leaf | 1 |
| 30 ml/2 tbsp white wine vinegar | 2 tbsp |
| 15-30 ml/1-2 tbsp sugar | 1-2 tbsp |
| ground ginger, to finish | |

Cook the onions gently in their skins in simmering salted water. Drain and peel them. Heat the oil, cloves, peppercorns and bay leaf in a fryng pan. Add the onions and let them simmer for about 6 minutes. Add the vinegar and sugar and simmer again until the liquid is reduced and syrupy.

Serve with a little sprinkling of ginger.

# Rice with a golden crust
### (Timman)
### Serves 4-8

| METRIC/IMPERIAL | U.S. |
|---|---|
| 450 g/1 lb Basmati rice | 2 ⅔ cups |
| 1.7 litre/3 pints water | 7½ cups |
| 125 g/4½ oz butter, preferably clarified | 9 tbsp |
| fine sea salt | |

As rice is such an important part of Middle Eastern meals, it is usual to serve greater quantities than in the West. At Jonquil's home in Baghdad, rice was often served at lunch with green beans or okra in tomato sauce. She often watched her aunts preparing the rice — always with great care.

Hakaka, the name for the crust which forms at the bottom of the pan, was a great favourite, and she and her sister would pounce hungrily on these golden pieces. This recipe was sent by her father from Baghdad.

Soak the rice in warm water for 20 minutes, then drain.
Bring the salted water to the boil and add 15 g/½ oz (1 tbsp) of butter. Add the rice slowly. Cook for about 7 minutes or until the water has almost all been absorbed. Drain the rice in a sieve.
In a clean saucepan, melt half the remaining butter, add the rice and cook on a high heat for 3-4 minutes. Then turn down the heat to very low. Dot the remaining butter, in little pieces, over the surface of the rice. Cover the saucepan, putting a clean cloth under the lid to prevent condensation from the steam dripping into the rice. Leave to cook for 35 minutes or until the grains of rice are dry.
When ready to serve, fill the bottom of the sink with cold water.
Take the pan from the heat and plunge its base into the cold water. There will a tremendous noise and much steam, but don't be alarmed; all will be well. Leave the rice for 5-7 minutes, then either unmould it upside down onto a plate, or spoon the rice into a bowl and add pieces of the golden Hakaka.

# Leek and potato purée with cheese
(Papet vaudois)
Serves 4-6

| METRIC/IMPERIAL | U.S. |
|---|---|
| 900 g/2 lb leeks | 2 lb |
| 900 g/2 lb potatoes | 2 lb |
| fine sea salt and freshly ground black pepper | |
| 100 g/4 oz Gruyère cheese | ¼ lb |
| dash of wine vinegar | |

Cut the leeks into 2.5 cm/1 inch chunks, including as much of the green part as is possible. Wash thoroughly. Peel the potaotes and cut into 2.5 cm/1 inch chunks. Simmer together with the leeks in boiling salted water for 30-35 minutes or until very soft.

Drain the vegetables, then mash together until they resemble a purée of potatoes. Mix in the grated cheese and the vinegar, with salt and pepper to taste.

An alternative version is to halve the amount of potatoes, and to cook the vegetables in a mixture of white wine and water.

# Celeriac and potato purée
(Purée de céleri-rave)
Serves 4

| METRIC/IMPERIAL | U.S. |
|---|---|
| 350-450 g/¾-1 lb celeriac | ¾-1 lb |
| fine sea salt and freshly ground black pepper | |
| 225 g/8 oz potatoes | ½ lb |
| 50 g/2 oz butter/vegetable margarine | 4 tbsp |
| milk or single (light) cream | |

A vegetable that accompanies venison to perfection.

Peel the celeriac, cut into chunks and immediately immerse in a pan of salted water (if you do not the celeriac will begin to go brown and look most unpleasant). Bring to the boil and simmer until tender; drain well. Peel the potatoes and cook in boiling salted water until tender; drain.

Purée the vegetables together with the butter in a mixer or blender — not in a food processor or you will end up with glue! Put the purée into a non-stick saucepan and heat slowly, then add a little milk or cream and lots of pepper.

# Short pastry (1)
Makes about 350 g/12 oz

| METRIC/IMPERIAL | U.S. |
| --- | --- |
| 225 g/8 oz plain (all-purpose) flour | 1 ⅔ cups |
| pinch of fine sea salt | |
| 100 g/4 oz butter | 1 stick |
| 1 egg yolk, optional | 1 |
| iced water to bind | |

Sift the flour and salt into a bowl. Rub the butter lightly into the flour, using only the finger tips, until it has the texture of fine breadcrumbs. Add the egg yolk, if using, and enough iced water to bind to a stiff dough. Be careful not to add too much liquid. Cover and chill until required.

# Short pastry (2)
Makes about 350 g/12 oz

| METRIC/IMPERIAL | U.S. |
| --- | --- |
| 100g /4 oz vegetable margarine suitable for | |
| pastry-making | ½ cup |
| 45 ml/3 tbsp water | 3 tbsp |
| 225 g/8 oz plain (all-purpose) flour | 1 ⅔ cups |
| pinch of fine sea salt | |

Place the margarine, water and 30 ml/2 tbsp of flour in a bowl and cream together with a fork until mixed. Add the remaining flour and continue mixing with a fork to form a firm dough. Knead on a lightly floured surface until firm and smooth. Cover and chill until required.

# INDEX